A FEARLESS GUIDE

to Starting a

Profitable 5K Business

Create Immediate Income by
Investing $5,000 or Less

MARILYN SWEET

Cherry Creek Press
Boulder, CO
www.5KBiz.com

Cherry Creek Press
Boulder, CO 80301

Publisher's Cataloging-in-Publication
(Provided by Quality Books, Inc.)

> Sweet, Marilyn, 1949-
>   A fearless guide to starting a profitable 5K business
>   : create immediate income by investing $5,000 or less /
> Marilyn Sweet. -- 1st ed.
>   p. cm.
>   Includes index.
>   ISBN-13: 978-0-9785720-0-6
>   ISBN-10: 0-9785720-0-9
>
>   1. Small business--Management. 2. New business
> enterprises--Management. 3. Self-employed.   I. Title.

    HD62.7.S99 2006   658.02'2
                                QBI06-600225

We are the sum total of everyone we have known
and all who love us.
Books are a reflection of the influence of numerous people
from our present and past.
These people make my world better and brighter.
I thank them every day for sharing their lives with me.
They are, without question, the best part of my life.

Dedicated to my parents, Dorothy Ogg Sweet and Arthur Sweet, Rest in Peace

To My Family
Rita, for her unwavering love and devotion,
my wonderful brothers: Norman and David who have always supported
me and my projects, and Sadie and Rosie for patiently waiting for their
walks

Acknowledgements

Special thanks to Carol Dovi O'Dywer for giving guidance, encouragement and enthusiasm liberally and often during this project.

Thank you to Beth Wienski and Cynthia Kowert for over 20 years of amazing friendship and support, along with Judy Jones, Susan Horigan, Jackie June, Kathleen June, May Lowry, Sam Horn, and many others who contributed their concern, time, and ideas.

Table of Contents

Introduction to the 5K Biz Model

Want to know the truth about starting a business? Many people make it too hard. They spend too much money. All too often, they don't make any money.

I have started eight businesses over the last 25 years and spent less than $5,000 each time. In fact I even retired at 51 from my regular job because I was able to fully fund my retirement accounts with income from my after-hours 5K businesses. Currently my "5K Biz" provides extra income so I do not need to tap any of the savings in my retirement accounts. I never wrote a business plan, took out a business loan, or had any debt. My businesses made money immediately.

You can fund your pre-retirement or retirement income with a 5K Biz too. Or, if you're a stay-at-home parent, you can contribute to your family's income and avoid the day care and commuting nightmare. You can grow it into a full-time job that you love. Your 5K Biz should make money for you right away too. Let me show you how.

If you want to pursue your passion and get paid to do the work you love, this book will start you on your path. Unlike your typical How-To-Start-a-Business book, this guide focuses on easily implemented techniques that have worked for me and my clients.

I share real-life stories of people just like you who are now living their dream because they dared to stop wishing and start acting.

You'll learn innovative, proven ideas that will help you launch your 5K Biz and ensure its success including how to:

- Quickly evaluate your idea to determine if it will accomplish your desired goals
- Use the new IRS tax deduction to help pay for start up costs for your business
- Spur your business to success by separating yourself from the competition by introducing the Value Added Benefit
- Generate enough revenue to pay yourself a handsome salary and earn a high Return On Investment
- Project a corporate image without paying expensive monthly rent, staff salaries or other overhead costs (pay less than $50 for a professional logo).
- Set up a low-cost advertising strategy that effectively targets the clients you want to reach
- Recruit a hidden sales force that will work for you 24-7 without costing you a dime with an easy-to-use strategy.
- Enjoy marketing your business even though you "hate" sales
- Avoid trial-and-terror learning as the author shares the mistakes she made starting eight companies (they succeeded in spite of her mistakes, so imagine how much more successful you could be by learning how to avoid them!)
- Set up your marketing plan with the innovative Core Marketing approach and learn how to recruit great customers who pay you well for your expertise and highly value your product
- Read about people just like you who have created their dream job that give them the freedom to pursue their interests and passions.

Now let's get started learning about the possibilities for your future business that will increase your income and peace of mind.

1 Profiting From Your Passion

It was a beautiful fall day in September 2002. My friend, Carol, and I were hiking up a trail in the Arapahoe National Forest outside of Vail, Colorado. The aspens were turning gold and the sunshine was warm on our faces. Soon we would snowshoe this trail but, for now, it was easy hiking.

I was deep in thought. Income tax time was coming. I opened a part-time income tax preparation business in November of 2000 and then retired from my full- time job as a psychologist in May 2001 at age 51. After two years of doing taxes, I wanted a new business that would be more personally satisfying to me.

"So how is the new business going?" asked Carol.

"Well, its okay but I want to try something new," I said.

"I can't believe you. What could be better than working 4 months and having the rest of the year off?" she said.

"I like doing income taxes but I get more enjoyment talking with my clients about financial matters. I want a business that gets me more involved with the clients," I said. "And I want to work more of the year. I was bored this summer."

"You always have to have a new project, don't you? What do you want to do now?" she asked.

"I am opening a mortgage company," I said.

"Another mortgage company? Are you crazy? There are a million mortgage companies! I get postcards and calls from them all the time. They drive me crazy," she exclaimed.

"There are 1,277 mortgage companies in the Yellow Pages to be exact but my plan is to give people more of what they want. They may not know they want more but they do," I said.

"What does that mean?" she asked.

"When I was renovating houses in Denver and getting mortgages, the loan officers never explained all the options to me. I am an information person and they didn't add to my information base about financing options. I would have liked to have learned more about how mortgages are priced and the options available. I believe people will appreciate a company that gives them information to make better decisions. In my opinion, mortgage companies underestimate their clients," I explained.

"You're right. My mortgage person hardly said anything to me about other types of mortgages or pricing. It would have been nice to learn a little bit about what I was doing. Maybe you have a good concept," she said.

"Also the name Boulder Mortgage Company is available. The previous owner just released it from ownership so I grabbed it. Getting this name was very important to making the decision to start the company. Having this name will give me an edge when I advertise. People love living in Boulder and the name is a classic," I said.

"Wow, that is a great name. It is a timeless name for your company. I love it. It's a sign that you should have this company," she exclaimed.

"A logo with the Flatiron Mountains will look great on business cards. I'm having a logo drawn too," I said.

"Isn't it expensive to have a custom logo? I heard they are thousands of dollars!" she said.

"I found a great deal for logos and it's only costing $35 for the drawing," I said.

"It will cost thousands of dollars to have an office and secretary. I thought you wanted to have a flexible schedule," Carol said.

"I won't be going into an office. I found some interesting alternatives to having an office and a staff. I want to design my business to suit me not just copy everybody else," I said.

"You have done some terrific research on this. You'll be great at mortgages. Everyone we know always asks you for advice on financial matters. 'What would Marilyn do?' is the first question my friends ask when they are thinking of a new project or business," she laughed.

"Is that why they are always calling me with questions? Maybe that's another business idea!" I said. Little did I know that not only would I start charging for that advice, it led to writing this book.

How to Turn Your Interests Into Serious Income With the 5K Business Model

When I started exploring writing a book on this topic, I discovered that the start-your-own business books currently on the market fell into two categories: those that require a substantial investment and ones that require no investment. The Small Business Administration defines a small business as having less than 1500 employees so many books try to address that market. On the other extreme are business startup books that require no initial outlay of money from the new owners, or so called "shoestring" businesses.

Unfortunately starting a business on a shoestring often results in undercapitalized businesses that lack the basic resources to market their services and meet their customer's needs. In particular, shoestring businesses do not allow for spending money on advertising which is essential to succeed in the business world. Even a minimal advertising budget will greatly increase your chances for making a substantial income from your new venture. Many shoestring businesses actually fall into the "hobby" category, which provides little or no income.

Conversely, starting a business that requires employees, renting office or warehouse space, and buying equipment is a tremendous financial and personal risk for most fledgling business owners. Getting a business loan is a huge undertaking and extremely costly in terms of monthly overhead to pay back that high interest loan. New owners are often unaware of the vast amount of advertising and marketing dollars required to support loan payments, rent and utilities, employee payroll, and salaries every month. The most common comment I hear is, "I never knew how much it costs to advertise." Many businesses fail due to being "undercapitalized," which means they ran out of money.

I realized there was a middle ground between these two extremes that wouldn't require people to invest their life savings but would show them how to develop a successful business with a modest outlay and low overhead. A budget of $5,000 allows the owner to buy essential equipment and present a professional image along with a modest advertising budget to get started. I call it the *5K Business Model or 5K Biz.*

The 5K business requires less than a $5,000 investment to begin earning revenue. Earning money immediately, without having to pay a lot of overhead bills, means more money in your pocket. It means less stress. It means being able to concentrate on your business to develop it to be a business you will enjoy.

And, as a bonus, the IRS recently changed the rule on startup business costs and now allows you to deduct $5,000 for your new business before you start earning money. So you can get all the equipment and supplies you need to start and deduct the costs from next year's taxes.

A 5K business does not mean you will only earn $5,000 a year. I have started 8 different businesses and my current business earns over $100,000 a year. I have helped many clients start their 5K businesses and most are successful and earning satisfying salaries.

Here are some typical 5K businesses:

- Home Handyman
- Personal Trainer
- Accountant
- Lawyer
- Mortgage Broker
- House Cleaner
- Lawn and Garden Specialist
- Lawn Mowing Service
- Lawn Sprinkler Installation and Repair
- Interior Decorator
- Real Estate Agent
- Real Estate Appraiser
- Consultants for Many Different Industries
- Home Energy Analysis
- Magazine Article Writer
- Electrician
- Plumber
- Collectible Reseller
- Ebay Seller
- Website Designer
- Tax Preparer
- Pet Groomer
- Virtual Assistant
- Personal Assistant
- Corporate Trainer
- Professional Speaker
- Pet Sitter and Dog Walker

Many people start their 5K business as a part-time business. They "practice" their business on weekends and nights before quitting their full-time jobs or retiring. This allows them to learn the basic skills of owning a business such as bookkeeping, income tax requirements, inventory control, ordering materials, and setting their prices. *When the owners become full time or retired, they know how much money they can make and have the additional advantage of no business loan payments.* They have practiced their trade and have confidence in their ability to deliver great products and services to their customers. Knowing the pitfalls of your business before you have to live on the income is a priceless advantage over your competition.

My 5K business clients have been from all walks of life and situations. I have helped stay-at-home moms and dads, the newly fired, almost retired, already retired, and the I-need-to-get-out-of-my-job-now types, both young and old, find a fulfilling business. You may be like me and start several part time 5K businesses during your working career and, after retirement, start a full-time business with flexible hours that provide you with enough money to truly enjoy your retirement.

Further benefits of the 5K business model are:

- Pursue your passion and use your personal knowledge as a Value Added Benefit to your customers' experience.
- Change your service or product as you learn more about your customers and the business. A 5K business can add or delete services as needed quickly and efficiently.
- Start on a part-time basis and test the market before committing to investing major money.
- You do not need to write a business plan. It is, however, important to have definite ideas about the steps needed to develop your business.
- You do not need to take out loans to pay for a store or inventory. Many businesses are able to begin generating

revenues with the $5,000 start up money.

- If you wish to become a large company, you are free to pursue that without the burden of loans and you will know your customer base.
- Advertising can be focused and unique by highlighting the Added Value Benefit you provide.
- Price your product or service competitively since you do not have the overhead of your competitors.
- Learn how to run a business by learning the skills you need such as bookkeeping and inventory slowly.
- Not having to meet a payroll every week is a luxury that allows you to experiment with different ideas and products.
- Starting your 5K Biz part-time while you are working is a great way to fund your IRA or Roth IRA accounts to the maximum allowed.
- Continuing your business after retirement means you can delay tapping into your retirement accounts for several years thus allowing your savings to grow.

Here's an example of a new 5K business:

Larry was a teacher with two children and needed more income. He began a small lawn mowing service in the summers. He bought a used trailer, a gas trimmer, and a professional level lawn mower and spent $4,500. Larry distributed flyers in local neighborhoods.

Larry loved mowing lawns and being outdoors so it was a natural fit for him. He liked talking to his neighbors about their lawns and felt a sense of pride seeing a beautiful green lawn.

Larry mowed my lawn every week and I often saw him run to his truck to grab a handful of fertilizer or seed to put on a bad patch in my yard. He carried a sprinkler wrench in his back pocket and would adjust the sprinkler heads if needed. Several times, Larry used a hand aerator to improve a small section of my lawn.

Larry cared about my lawn more than I did. He loved seeing improvement in his client's lawns. Even though it took him only three or four minutes to do these minor jobs, I was grateful for his caring attitude.

After the first summer Larry never had to advertise again and had to turn down new customers because of his attention to his customer's lawns. He raised his rates 25 percent, hired some additional help and was soon making a significant amount of money every summer. He has a sterling reputation and is thinking of expanding his business to include installing sprinkler systems.

Why Do I Advise Starting With $5,000?

You might be wondering why I chose $5,000 as the money needed for start up costs. For me, spending $5,000 is a serious decision. I will be careful and will research my options before committing that much money. I want my readers to do the same careful consideration before beginning a new venture.

Setting aside $5,000 means that you will have enough money to buy some basic equipment to get started. You will be able to have a logo designed for you, set up a computer system, and buy the necessary software to present a professional image. And you will be able to deduct all the costs on your income tax return which is a nice perk from the IRS.

In addition, your business will have the capital to advertise for several months so that you can begin making money immediately. *Neglecting to advertise and market your business is the number one reason for small business failure.* You must start your business with a plan to attract customers.

Use Your Know-How to Develop Your Ideal Business

Discovering the perfect business is an ongoing process of capitalizing on the skills you've acquired both on your job and off your job, and then believing that your pastime can be profitable. Larry, for instance, had developed great relationships skills as a teacher who nurtured his students' talents. By coupling his outstanding attentive skills with his love for lawn keeping, he was able to develop a successful business with a minimal investment.

Many people assume that what they enjoy outside of a 9-5 job—their hobbies, passions and interests--cannot be turned into a profitable business because it is too idealistic and not an attainable goal. They assume that they will need to commute to a corporate job, will always have a boss, and do work that they do not enjoy.

Unless they challenge their belief system or something changes in their life to upset these preconceived notions, they may never venture beyond this corporate security. Sometimes it takes a major shakeup in our lives—what we first perceive as a loss—to open our eyes up to our gifts and convince ourselves that we can do what we love for a living.

My friend, Dan, had always worked for others. He was a stable provider for his wife and two teenage children. When he was laid off at age 47 from a commercial real estate firm, he was in shock. His position had seemed secure and he expected to retire from the company. Dan had never enjoyed his work very much but was a diligent, competent worker. He suspects he was replaced by a younger and lower paid employee even though the company said they were cutting back every department.

Dan had a small collection of toy model trains. This collection was his passion and even though his collection wasn't large, it was of very high quality. He had studied the market since he was very young and knew literally everything about collecting model trains. Dan was well known in the small world of model train collectibles and often wrote short articles for some websites.

The local model train collectible storeowner was a friend and offered him a job. Dan knew he could not afford to work for a store clerk's wages but wanted to be in the collectible business if he could. Even as Dan was looking for work in commercial real estate, he began going to auctions, in person and online, and buying select pieces.

He set up an Ebay sellers account and began reselling some of the items he found. Slowly he developed a following and collectors paid him to find special items. His new Web site has a newsletter, advice column and paid subscribers. His income is increasing every month.

Dan found another job in real estate but is now working part time from home for this new company in a specialty area. He doesn't make as much money as his previous job but is enjoying this new position.

His fledgling model train business is growing and he hopes to eventually become a full-time model consultant. He learned that he enjoys writing a newsletter and several companies are interested in buying some articles to add to their advertising materials. Dan knows that, at the very least, he will have a good business to pursue after he retires that will add income and enjoyment to his life.

Little did Dan expect that he could make a living doing what he loved. Do you have a hobby or activity that makes your soul sing? Have you considered turning your passion into a profession? Even if your hobby is like Dan's with a seemingly small audience, it is worth exploring how you can build a small business from your knowledge and enthusiasm.

Thousands of people have discovered that once they acted on their belief that their special interests and talents could be turned into income, they began to live the life they wanted and pursue work they enjoyed. Do some informal research. Look in the Yellow Pages listings under your hobby or interest and look at the businesses listed. You may find that other people have found a way to earn income from your hobby. Call the business and see the services or products they offer. Use the ideas in this book to formulate a plan for yourself so that you can have the advantages that comes form making your passion into a small business.

Developing a Value Added Benefit

When considering entering the highly competitive mortgage business, *I realized that there were services I could add to the customer's experience that would set my company apart.* My experiences with the many mortgage companies I dealt with during my real estate investor years were generally poor to fair. I did not get any guidance or TLC, Tender Learning Care, from the loan officers about mortgages. They just wrote the application and processed the loan. They didn't do a bad job but they didn't impress me either.

After learning about the intricacies of the mortgage industry, I was amazed none of the loan officers took the time to advise me. I was an investor and an excellent prospect for more mortgages. But because they did not go that extra step to earn my appreciation and trust, I felt no loyalty to their company and was unlikely to return to do business with them again or most importantly refer my friends to them. This experience prompted me to develop a Value Added Benefit for my new business.

The Value Added Benefit gives the customer more than they anticipated. For many businesses, the Value Added Benefit provides the customer with additional knowledge about the service or product.

The Value Added Benefit pleasantly surprises your client and demonstrates your generosity and appreciation for their business. Provide TLC, Tender Learning Care, and you'll have happy customers and a profitable company.

Having a memorable Value Added Benefit means your customers will sell your services for you. They turn into a 24/7 sales force for you.

For example:

- Dan helps model train collectors add quality pieces to increase the value of their collections and provides recommendations on their next steps. He shows interest in their goals and suggests ideas about how to focus their collections in a particular way to make them more valuable or unique.
- Larry leaves a note for each customer suggesting ways to improve their lawns and offers a free consultation. He does small improvement jobs when he is mowing their lawns. His caring attitude makes a strong impression on his customers.
- Accountants provide client specific suggestions for saving money on next year's taxes and discuss ways to rearrange their deductions for maximum advantage.
- A mortgage company discusses a creative way to finance a home based on the customer's plans for the future. For example, a loan officer suggests a loan that would be paid off by retirement.

In all cases, the Value Added Benefit is not a way to sell more services. Already many customers feel like they are being hooked and reeled in by companies who pretend to care but are really setting them up for a larger bill. When you give the client your time and knowledge, it is without charge. You show them that you have their best interests in mind.

Finding Your Unique Value Added Benefit

Here's how I helped one of my clients discover her Valued Added Benefit:

May wants to become a real estate agent and called me to discuss the realities of the profession. She is married and is mom to a preschooler, Samantha. She loves houses and she has a sharp eye for decorating and color. Her friends love her house that she decorated with very little money.

May and her husband have a large circle of friends and acquaintances so she hopes to get lots of referrals. She and her husband would like to eventually become investors in real estate as part of their retirement portfolio.

Marilyn, I know you were a real estate agent in the 1990s. What's the best way to get started with this business? What could be a Value Added Benefit for me to help my customers?

May, you would be a great agent. Keep in mind that the competition is intense for business. Having a large circle of friends is helpful but let's develop a Value Added Benefit for you. The Value Added Benefit will make your clients glad they hired you to help them sell their house and distinguish you from all the other agents.

Okay, that sounds good. But I have no idea what to offer. It seems like everything that's possible to do in real estate has already been done. I see all the ads by the well-known agents. What could I do to compete with them?

You told me one reason you would be an agent is because you have an eye for recognizing quick and appealing changes that would make the home sell faster.

That's true. I watch the cable show "Sell This House" and I can predict what the professionals are going to say about the house they are trying to sell. One reason people like my home is that it is decorated with clean lines. But don't all agents already do that as part of their service?

In my experience, many agents give information to their clients about getting a house ready to sell. But they generally hand the client a packet with information. What if you went the extra step and helped them see their house as others would see it?

Gee, that's a good idea. And I would love doing that. I could advertise that I will help them prepare their houses for showings. Maybe we could watch a tape of one of the "Sell This House" shows so they could see what a difference it makes to organize their home. Then we could walk around their house and work on different rooms.

That would be a great service to many people. Did you know that there are professional home stagers? But many people don't want to spend more money to sell their homes. The key to this service is that you are *spending time with them* and showing how much you care that their home sells quickly and profitably. You could also have phone numbers for reliable handy men, storage facilities and lawn care companies if they need some additional help.

This makes me want to get started. I feel like I really have something to market to clients. This is a great Value Added Benefit, and I think it will be my favorite part of the job. I feel very comfortable offering this service. Thanks for your help.

Don't forget that your decorator's sense of color and style will be invaluable for folks buying a new house too. You can help them see a hidden gem in a house that's painted bright orange. And show them how to arrange a room so the sofa fits.

You can advise them about houses with poor floor plans that will not accommodate their furniture. Be sure to take before and after pictures of homes you help to stage so your potential clients can see visual proof of your talents. Make notes about the costs too.

Wow! Great idea! I have before and after pictures of my own home and the cost breakdown of the remodeling. I will get started with a staging book now. Thanks for everything.

One caution however. Be sure to offer a limited amount of time for the staging advice such as one to two hours for the free service. You want your time to be valued.

Oh, that is important. I love the idea but I need to make money too. I'll have to monitor myself. I can get carried away with my enthusiasm and give away my knowledge for free. Thanks for the warning.

By capitalizing on her accumulated knowledge and natural talent, May has a good start to her new business. Developing her Value Added Benefit as the main selling point for her new business will help increase her confidence in her new business and make it stand out from other real estate agents. *It's much easier to begin a new venture when you feel comfortable and confident in your value to your clients.* You will be more relaxed talking with new prospects. Having a prop like a design book with before and after pictures of staged homes is a unique approach to marketing that will help set you apart from the competition.

These examples show how you can develop your unique Value Added Benefit for your business idea. Ask your friends to help. They know you well and can help you define skills that will enhance your business.

You will find that you will more aware of the good practices that other businesses use as you purchase products and services for your family. You will notice the extra effort a business provides and be more appreciative of their service. Adding these extra touches to your business will increase your chances for success.

Conversely, you will also be aware of businesses that are doing a poor job with customers. Notice the difference in how you feel about a business who is trying to do a better job and the business that has poor customer service. That positive feeling is why you return to a business. Be sure to incorporate as many good practices in your business as possible.

Tweaking Your Business Concept for Success

Carol and I met again for another hike on the same trail in the Arapahoe Forest in March 2004. This time we were on snowshoes and seeing bare trees instead of golden aspens. The weather was clear and cold with a brilliant ice blue sky.

"Your mortgage company idea turned out to be very profitable. I hardly talked with you all last year. I thought you retired in 2001, but it looks like you are busier than ever. So much for "retirement"," Carol laughed.

"The mortgage company exceeded my wildest dreams, that's for sure. I think everyone in the country refinanced their mortgage in 2003," I said.

"Did your ideas about designing your business work out?" Carol asked.

"I had to modify a few things as I went along. But I never

had to sit in an office all day waiting for customers to come in and that was my goal. I hired an assistant for a while but she worked out of her home too. The fax machine is a wonderful invention along with email," I said.

"It's hard to believe that you never rented a full time office with a secretary and all the trappings and still had lots of customers. But everyone we know has refinanced with you and loved the service so I guess the traditional office setup isn't that important," Carol said.

"Apparently it isn't," I said.

"You've had a few businesses since I've known you. Is the mortgage business your most successful?" asked Carol.

"Actually my first business was the most profitable. I had a tutoring business when I was in grad school and made enough money to pay all my tuition and living expenses," I said.

"What did you tutor?" she asked.

"I tutored Advanced Statistics and Research Design. All grad students had to take it and pass a comprehensive exam to get their degree. I invented an easy system to explain the concepts and decided to tutor others because I was extremely poor at the time," I explained.

"Statistics! What a horrible course that was for me! I never did understand any of it. I just bluffed my way through it. I'm not sure my instructor knew it either. What a great subject to tutor. Bet you had a lot of business," Carol said.

"I had grown men almost crying on the phone to get into my group. I ended up having groups of 12 to 14 students and they paid me $12 an hour so I earned $144 plus per hour. In 1983, that was serious money. The beauty of the business was that I never had to advertise and I used empty classrooms to hold group session. It was the ideal business. Since then I've been trying to recreate that profit level and freedom to choose my customers," I explained.

"Well, $144 an hour is serious money today too! Did every-one pass the exam?" she asked.

"Yes, it was wildly successful. My next 5 businesses were not as lucrative but each one taught me valuable lessons," I said.

Here's what I learned about myself and the art of business from tutoring that led me to develop the successful 5K business model:

- Keeping your advertising and office space costs low means more profit in your pocket.
- I loved explaining difficult concepts in terms people could understand and was quite good at this. As a result, I not only developed a new way to teach statistics that worked, I've gone on to develop other businesses in which I explain difficult concepts, like mortgage financing and income taxes for instance, in easy-to-understand terms to my customers.
- Realizing that I could come up with good ideas gave me confidence in my ability to develop marketable businesses. This proved to be critical to my future.
- I loved communicating my sincere concern to my students, which led them to recommend my tutoring services to their fellow students. Being sincerely interested in the outcome of my students was inspiring to me.
- It was rewarding and personally satisfying to be responsible for my own success which motivated me to continue to start my own businesses.
- Making money was very important and gratifying to me. It was possible for me at age 29 to make $144 an hour. This led me to believe that I could be a highly paid person. And as you will see later in my book, developing confidence in your ability to do something well, like create a thriving business, is the first step in achieving success.

2 Don't Just Escape, Make an Exit Plan

When you're desperate to leave your present job it is difficult to assess opportunities accurately. Every chance at getting out of your current situation seems like a good idea. Each business for sale appears to be just the right business for you and your family. Every pitch from the salesman seems to answer the exact questions and concerns you are having.

That's how people get into trouble. Instead of developing a plan for a company that fits their values and uses their natural knowledge about a product or service, they latch unto someone else's dream. Instead of asking smart questions to evaluate the feasibility of a new venture, they fall for a too-good-to-be-believed sale pitch. Here's how my friend Sara almost got taken and how you can avoid falling into similar traps by making an exit plan for a 5K business that suits your talents and interests and meets your priorities.

My good friend Sara called on a Friday night with an interesting request. She wanted my advice.

"Marilyn, will you go to the Franchise Show with me at the Denver Merchandise Mart tomorrow?" my friend Sara asked.

"Sure, I'd love to see what types of franchises are being offered these days," I said.

"I am desperate to find another job," said Sara. "I'm 42 and I have been a teacher for 20 years. I still love the kids but the paperwork, meetings, and exhaustion are getting to me. I just don't think I can continue working sixty to seventy hours a week from August to May any longer."

"Do you have any specific ideas on what you are looking for?" I asked.

"I saw a couple of franchises that look promising to me and I'd like your opinion on them," she replied.

I agreed and the next morning we drove to the Merchandise Mart and were immediately assaulted with a 100 franchise businesses trying to get our attention.

The first business Sara was interested in was a vending machine business. A large crowd had gathered in front of the booth.

"Do you all drink soda? Eat M&M's?" bellowed the salesman.

"Yes!" shouted many in the crowd.

"We all drink soda and get snacks at work, don't we?" shouted the salesman.

"How about making some real money while you sleep, while you're picking your kids up from school, while you're on vacation?" another saleswoman said.

"I'm making $300,000 a year with these machines and only working about 20 to 25 hours a week. I make money while I sleep!" declared Bob the salesperson. "Let me show you the easy life. These state-of-the-art machines will give you hundreds of dollars a week in cash. Buy the soda wholesale, stock the machines, and a week later you'll have made hundreds of dollars just for restocking the soda and scooping up all that money. And you'll make this money week after week. Hire a friend to do the stocking and you're off on your vacation. And it's making money for you while you're on the beach. What

could be easier than that?"

"Where do you put the machines?" someone in the crowd asked.

"We have thousands of businesses waiting for these machines in Denver and we will find the locations for you. You can have your own business and work the hours you want to work," shouted Bob. There was a large crowd around Bob by now eagerly listening

"How many machines do I need to buy to make $300,000 a year?" asked a woman.

"Well, you'll need five or six machines to make that kind of money. If you don't have the cash to invest in your business, we'll help you get started with a small business loan. After the loan is paid, all the cash you make is yours," he said.

"How much do you have to pay these companies to put the machines in their offices and shops?" another man asked.

"You pay ZERO. They are happy to have these new machines in their lunchrooms. If you are interested in hearing more about this incredible opportunity, come with me. We can only offer this to the first 20 people, so sign up over here with Bob. We will drive you to our private offices so you can see at how you can make $100,000, $200,000 even $300,000 extra a year in your spare time," shouted the saleswoman.

Sara turned to me eagerly. "Should I sign up? What do you think? They only take 20 people per day," she said.

"Sara, let's step over here and discuss this before you go anywhere with them. First, I remember reading that Denver Public Schools makes $1,500,000 a year with their soda machines. Why would any business let you put a machine in their lunchroom, use their electricity, heat, and floor space for nothing? Why wouldn't they buy their own machines and earn some money on them?" I said.

"Hmm, now I remember that my school makes money from

the pop machines too and uses it for the copy machine costs. I guess they aren't telling the whole story on that. Is anything else wrong with this idea?" she asked.

"Well, I find it very hard to believe that there are thousands of businesses waiting for these machines. Again, why wouldn't they just buy their own machines? The real story on most vending machine companies is that the machines actually cost these salespeople about $2,000 and they sell them to you for $5,000. So they make money but you have a machine that you cannot sell for what you paid for it. Let's look up vending machine companies on the Internet when we get home before you commit to anything." I said.

"Okay I think you are right. I was ready to go sign up. I <u>want</u> to believe that there is a part-time business that will pay me $100,000 a year I guess," said Sara dejectedly.

"Let's look at the next franchise you liked before we leave," I said.

We strolled down a few aisles and stopped at a printing company's booth. They had a very innovative printing press that could print a logo or saying on just about anything. It was a very clever machine and small enough to put in a spare room in your house. The salesman did not make outrageous claims about making fabulous money. Sara thought this was very clever and that lots of businesses would like their logo on unusual things like walnuts. In minutes she was swept up with the excitement of this seemingly easy money-making opportunity.

I turned to my friend and quietly asked her, "So you have a burning desire to print logos?"

She looked at me in shock and after a moment of considering what she would be doing every day, with tears in her eyes and head down, whispered, "Marilyn, I just have to get out of my job."

Little did I know how many other people have been enticed into the vending machine business. A member of one of the focus groups reading the manuscript for this book admitted, sheepishly, that she had five new vending machines sitting in her basement. She was unable to find locations to place the machines after spending $30,000.

Assessing the Reality of Your Idea

To avoid making the kind of mistake my focus group member did, you need to first take a look at your life and dreams to find your new business. Do you have a hobby or pastime about which you have spent many years learning the fine points? Do your friends always call you for advice and depend on you for information in certain areas? Have you ever walked out of businesses offering the same or similar services and know you can do better for less money or at a higher quality? If so, you are now ready to begin thinking about how to fashion these ideas into reality.

Let's use some of the ideas from the first chapter to evaluate a real-life business idea. Here is a conversation I had about starting a new business, followed by six major questions you should ask yourself before you begin.

Rita is 52 and a corporate trainer in human resources. She has been doing private human resource training with a few clients for two years or so but always had a full-time job doing corporate training. She makes $55,000 a year. Rita is very close to an early retirement with a small pension and has always wanted to have her own business. She wants to earn $20,000 income from a business so she can travel and continue saving without touching any retirement savings. She doesn't want to dip into her retirement account to start a business, but she does have at least $5,000 in savings that she can easily ear-mark to invest.

Rita loves training employees and seeing the results. She is vivacious, energetic, and successful. The positive feedback from her private clients is extremely gratifying to her. She is looking forward to designing and creating individual training programs for companies. Rita has a passion and demonstrates a talent for the business she wants to start. Since she has always worked for somebody else, Rita has lots of questions about getting started.

Marilyn, what should I consider when I'm thinking about starting my 5K biz?

You want to consider these six main points:
1. How are you going to make money with your business? If you can't afford to leave your current employment, how can you start building your business part-time while keeping your job and eventually make the transition into self employment?
2. How much do you need to make per month to cover your overhead and expenses? What kind of salary do you want, and how much do you need?
3. What is the Value Added Benefit that your customers want and need?
4. How are you going to get new clients? Through advertising? Personal connections? Have you been able to sell your services to someone who doesn't know you?
5. How much can you invest in your business?
6. Do you want to eventually sell your business?

Okay let's see. Question 1 is: How am I going to make money with my business? I am getting national certification for my specialty, and I am doing some private consulting now. I have a professional contact and we are hoping to join forces. He is

a full-time consultant now, and he believes my skills and specialty will be very appealing to his clients.

Rita, will you be able to make enough money with these activities? How many days a month are you able to train? How much are you charging per day?

Let's see if I can figure that out. Question 2 is: How much do you need to make per month to cover your overhead and expenses? What kind of salary do you want and how much do you need?

Well, I have figured out that I will need about $2,000 clear a month to make it worth my time. My private contracts now pay about $800 a day, so four days a month would cover my salary and income taxes. I need to have some additional days to cover my overhead.

Great! Sounds like you have thought this out. First I would *develop a contract* to present to any company that asks you to do training. It should spell out all the details of your employment such as expenses you will be expected to cover at the contract price and the expenses the company will cover.

One question I would have is: *Does the company provide the meeting room, flyers, refreshments, copies, or any of the other incidentals trainers need?* Covering those expenses by the company puts more money in your pocket and makes the $800 a day more valuable to you.

Remember that you will be an independent contractor for any company that hires you to train employees. Your checks will not have any taxes subtracted, and each company will send you a Form 1099 for Miscellaneous Income at tax time. So you will be responsible for all the income tax and need to plan accordingly.

A great source for business people is www.nolo.com. This Web site has books that spell out in plain language all the important things to know about this type of contract. Most of the books come with a CD that has many typical agreements. You can customize a sample contract for independent contractors. Nolo explains all the income tax questions you will encounter. You should always consult an attorney for legal advice. Nolo will prepare you to ask your attorney the right questions and lower your legal consultation bill.

The next part of question 2 is: How much will my overhead be per month? I have no idea what my overhead will be.

Based on what you told me, $2,000 a month salary or $24,000 a year after expenses sounds realistic. You will have some additional benefits from your business such as deducting your car expenses, equipment deductions, and meals with clients or prospective clients.

I would aim for about $300 to $500 a month maximum overhead for the income level you have talked about earlier. Why $500 a month? For many 5K businesses, I believe that *overhead should ideally be no more than 20 percent* of your income. Keeping your overhead to a minimum means you can work less because you are paying less. Or you can work more and keep more money. That's the beauty of a 5K business. It keeps start-up costs and overhead low so you can pocket more of your income, and it gives you the flexibility to work as little or as much as you want, depending on your needs.

So the main goal now is to predict what expenses you will have and to *spend as little as possible without sacrificing any quality.* Let me ask you what are essential expenses you must spend to start this business?

I'll need a phone line, an office to meet clients and business cards, and that's about it I think.

Rita, I think you will find that you will have more expenses than this if you are going to have training sessions with corporations. How annoying is it to you when someone is speaking to a group and the microphone doesn't work? I feel as if they are not prepared and are wasting my time. It makes me mad.

I see what you mean. I hate that and see the presenter as incompetent. I would feel humiliated if my microphone kept cutting out. So I'll need a small audio system, overhead projector, and PowerPoint projector. Those are the machines I use most in my presentations.

I would advise that you *buy quality equipment with excellent reliability.* You will probably need about $2,000 to $3,000 for high quality equipment. Buy used whenever you can, especially if you have experience with a particular brand and know what you want.

(Check out Chapter 3 for ideas about making any large purchase and finding reviews that clue you into any flaws before you buy).

I think I need a nice office to compete with the other trainers out there who have more experience than me.

Do you want an office or do you think you *need* an office? I don't believe I have ever bought a service because the provider had a nice office. How do you make contact with your private clients now? Do they ask to meet you in your office?

Gee, actually they don't *ever* meet me in an office. We talk over the phone about their needs and I give them my programs and prices then I meet them at *their* office to see the training room. Maybe I don't need an office. I guess I'm feeling insecure about being on my own so an office feels like I'll have more credibil-

ity with them.

Many new business owners buy services and products based on their fear of being judged as amateurs. I can tell you from experience that many of your customers do not care about your office. Concentrate on *how* you are going to conduct your business rather than *where* you will conduct business. Some 5K business owners will need a full-time office (perhaps they have children or want to keep themselves accountable for regular office hours) and that's their preference.

However, offices are huge money wasters if you can do business without one. It means monthly rent, another phone bill, usually a DSL hookup, computer equipment, fax equipment, and office furniture. Most of us have all those things at home so an office requires duplication and is very expensive. I cannot live without a DSL line.

> *Of course to me, the worse thing about renting an office is having to go to the office. If I was paying $500 or more a month in rent for a small office, I would feel compelled to be there. Personally I do not want to work in an office if I can help it. Many 5K Business owners want to be free of not only the overhead of an office but also having to be in an office. They like the freedom to conduct business in a more personal and inexpensive way.*

That's a big relief. Monthly office rent was going to be a big expense.

That's one of the major benefits of the 5K Business Model. You can start a business with a moderate amount of money. It can be a challenge but a little research pays off with more money in your pocket. By the way, I am not an advocate of starting a business with no money, so called shoestring startups. This approach does not allow you to project a professional image and charge a reasonable fee for your services.

I can see why I don't need a monthly office, but how can I still project a high quality image?

How about a striking professional logo to go on your business cards and stationary? You'll be sending bids for training projects and flyers for coaching clients. A good logo really makes your company stand out from the crowd.

The good news is that you don't have to spend $1,000 on a pricey graphic artist and wait weeks. My custom color logo with motto for the mortgage company was $35 and was done in 4 days.

(Check out Chapter 3 for money saving tips on keeping your printing overhead incredibly low).

Okay. That sounds great. Now let's see. Question 3: What are my Value Added Benefits? Those would be many of the extra things I am doing now with my private customers. I feel strongly that the training should have a measurable impact on the workplace. I help my customers devise a survey and checklist so they can see if the training was effective. They love it and have told me no one else spends much time with them on this. We end up working together to make the next training even better. I love the collaboration and it's my favorite part of my business.

Terrific. You already have a strong and demonstrated Value Added Benefit as a basis for your successful business. It sounds like your clients think of you as a trusted advisor and that is the best position to be in as a consultant.

Be careful not to devote too much of your time to providing free Value Added Benefits. You could end up spending a disproportional amount of time on non-revenue producing activities. I suggest you have a specific amount of time you will give each client, such as a one-hour phone consultation that focuses specifically on helping your client develop a survey and checklist. You would then charge them for any time you spent reviewing their material. Free extras will "spur" your business ahead but you need to concentrate on making money. *The point of any business is to make money first.*

Marilyn, question 4 is: How am I going to get new clients?"

Rita, this is *the most critical step in starting and maintaining a business.* Having most of your livelihood depend on just one company or one referral source is very risky. Getting your own clients will be critical to your success. A company that is giving you $800 a day may need to cut back on their training budget next year. They will let you go in order to survive. There are no guarantees with self-employment status. This is why companies are willing to pay you more than they would an employee. It is to their advantage to have the flexibility to shed contractors with little notice or concern.

As your business grows, I would advise you to also hire independent contractors for those same reasons. First I would make sure you know the regulations for hiring independent contractors. Read your Nolo book carefully and talk with your attorney.

My advice is to make sure you have the demonstrated qualifications and certifications necessary to sell your training abilities or programs to other clients. You are already doing this by pursuing national certification. Then begin collecting positive references from paid training jobs. Start building a solid portfolio of satisfied customers. If you can afford it, a professional videographer using two cameras makes an appealing video presentation. Or negotiate with a client to have them videotape your presentation. Give them rights to use it for six months for new employees. You now have a well produced videotape to send to prospects or put on your Web site.

The more information you can give a prospective client the better. Your goal is to make the client feel totally comfortable about hiring you. Then you must have the confidence in yourself and the quality of the product and/or services you are offering. Offering quality services, being honest with your customers and earning their trust is more important than giving them the lowest quote,"

In addition to having qualifications, you will need to find a place to advertise and pay for the ads for 3 or 4 months. Do you have ideas about how to get more customers?

I have planned to do a postcard and letter campaign to all the companies I know and have worked with over the years. I have a database of contacts and will call them. Perhaps I could go to the library and get address of all the medium size businesses in the area and add them to my postcard list.

Great ideas. If you send a postcard, try to follow up with a call. Also get the names and addresses of meeting planners in your area. They would be good contacts for you too. You could invest in a direct mail campaign also. Sending postcards to meeting planners for conventions might also be a target market for you and well within your budget.

Ask your current customers for written recommendations. Include their comments on your website and ask a few customers if they would be willing to talk with a potential client.

Before you leave your job, you need to make contacts with people that can help you get corporate training jobs. Leaving your current position for an independent contractor position without knowing that there are customers for your own training business would be risky.

Join some general business and industry specific groups such as Society of Human Resource Mangers, American Society of Training and Development, and other Human Resource groups. Start offering to speak to business groups about your main training product and how it can help them in their business. You will need to make the talk informational and not just an advertisement for your product. Be careful about pitching your new business during these speaking engagements. It is a turnoff to most executives to be expecting an informative lecture and get a thirty-minute commercial with little useable information. If you help them, they will refer customers to you.

A wonderful book that will help you determine how to be an effective speaker and reap valuable extra benefits to boost your business is Dottie Walters' book, *Speak and Grow Rich*. This is a comprehensive book covering all aspects of professional speaking including setting fees. After you speak to a group, the attendees feel they know you and will remember your name.

Okay that sounds great. Now question 5: How much can I invest in my business? Well I have a lot saved for my retirement but I don't want to touch that. I think $3,000 to $5,000 amount is ideal for me.

I would try to set aside $5,000 for starting your business. Your concept fits perfectly with the 5K Business Model. Providing your own equipment will make your company seem more professional. I would not depend on any client to provide you with equipment. Having a projector or microphone that does not operate will make you look like an amateur and may ruin your training program not to mention your reputation.

The 6th question is: Do I want to eventually sell my business? Marilyn, right now I can't imagine I will have a good enough business that someone would want to buy it!

You would be surprised at how much a business like yours would be worth. If you expect to be in business for 10 to 15 years, your company will have built a reputation and a steady client list. You may have independent contractors doing training programs bringing in extra income. You will have records showing how much you have made per year, your overhead costs and tax returns with all the details. You will have equipment and valuable contacts at corporations and small businesses. It's not unlikely that your business income may be over $100,000 a year in several years. Anyone wanting to own a training company could buy your company and have a good income immediately. This is very attractive to many people.

For my mortgage company database, I keep track of all the loans I have done. I list not only the name and address for my mailing list but also the number of loans and loan amount, the date, referral source, and comments. A buyer looking at my list can easily see the advertising that has been most effective for me. Since the list is on a Microsoft Excel™ spreadsheet, the buyer can rearrange the loans to see what months and years I had the most loans. It is helpful to me also. I can identify my best referral sources and target my advertising dollars more effectively.

(Check out the section on Advertising in Chapter 5 for more tricks to save money and build your business).

> *To make your business more valuable to any buyer, you should have your business taxes professionally prepared every year. That's why I recommend that you have an accountant, preferably a CPA, on your team. A buyer will have more confidence in the gross income figures you are claiming if they can look at ten years of tax returns. They can check your overhead deductions and have a better idea of what their expenses will be. Valuing a business is tricky at best, and the more information you can provide the better. Your investment of $300 a year will pay off handsomely.*

Thanks for all your help, Marilyn. I feel better about starting this business and I'll begin my planning with your suggestions.

Selling Even If You Hate "Selling"

Once you've answered these questions, you need to think about your approach to sales. Few of us are natural sales people and often we had misgivings about our ability to sell. That's why I tell people:

Have a business product or service you believe in and are passionate about then you never have to sell anything. Just tell them what you believe.

And don't think you are the only one with sweaty palms.

Remember the client is nervous, too. They may be concerned that they will hire you for a training session and you will not do well. Their boss and co-workers will be upset with them. The more confident and reassuring you are, the easier it is to sell.

Think of what might be a concern to the client. Urge them to show the boss the video on your website. Ask them if your style would suit their company's workers. Give them names of referrals so they can ask questions privately. Most people are concerned about offending you. Answer their questions freely and honestly. If the training they want will not fit their goals, say so. They will remember you forever, and you can put them on your mailing list.

I often advise my callers to keep the mortgage they have rather than refinance. Now why would I do such a thing? I know that a sterling reputation of genuinely wanting to help my clients will be more valuable over the long haul than getting one sale. I always offer to watch the rates for them and ask for referrals to their friends.

By always giving your customers more than they expected, you set yourself apart from your competition and receive invaluable word-of-mouth advertising. When someone calls me about a mortgage, I tell them a couple of facts they probably didn't know about the mortgage industry: perhaps some information on how interest rates are calculated. Or I tell them the historical average of interest rates over the last twenty years. I spend time talking with them even though I know I may not have a sale with this client. Usually they thank me for my time, and I ask them to remember me for referrals to their friends. It takes ten minutes or less but makes a lasting impression.

In this way, I have established myself as an expert and as a trusted advisor. I am not an order taker. I am a professional who has their best interests at heart and will not lie to them. I disclose my compensation. I have even had several clients express concern that I am not making enough money when signing their loan closing papers. Now that's a compliment to any mortgage broker!

And don't assume that the lowest price quote is your customers' highest priority as illustrated by this example:

I had a handywoman come to my house to give me a bid on installing some insulation and a new sliding glass door. She checked on the insulation and said, "Your insulation is great and you don't need any more."

"Can you check the sliding glass door? It is very hard to slide it open," I said. She checked out the rollers and track and it was indeed very hard to roll. "I think this is worn out and the seal is broken," she said.

"Okay, how much do you think it could be?" I asked

She looked crestfallen and said, "You can get Home Depot to do the installation for a lower price than I can give you."

I said, "I want you to install it because I like supporting local businesses." She said she would price a door for me and get back to me. She never called me.

This small business owner assumed all I cared about was price. Maybe she was having a hard time financially and could not believe that I wanted a quality job rather than a cheap price. She did not have the confidence or perhaps the experience to realize that *customers have many different motives and price is often only one consideration.* She did not believe in the quality of her work and that others would value it. Every business owner I have talked to has said that when they were starting their business they automatically assumed that customers are only concerned with price. In many cases that assumption is not true.

Most customers want a quality service or product and are willing to pay more for that assurance. Selling is not hard or difficult if you believe in your service and yourself. Take the approach that the client has a problem to solve and that is why they have called you. You can either solve that problem or not. If you cannot, be honest with the customer. Advise the client of your opinion and offer to help them contact a more appropriate trainer.

> *Start a business providing a product or service you passionately believe in then you never have to sell anything. Just tell the customer what you believe.*

What's In a Name? Everything!

Business names are extremely important in my opinion. The name reflects you and your values. It is inexpensive advertising. I was lucky and snagged the name Boulder Mortgage Company for Boulder, Colorado, even though most people would assume that name was taken. Many older names become available when the original owner fails to renew the trademark.

> *A good place to search for trade names is your Secretary of State's business website. In Colorado, the SOS has a search engine that allows you to see if a business*

name is taken. I registered Boulder Mortgage Com-
pany and Aspen Mortgage Company for $50 each. I'm
not sure I will ever start an Aspen Mortgage Company,
but I have the rights to the name if I want to expand.
Register for the business name in your state so no one
else can use it.

Choose a name that says something positive about your business. I have a bias against company names that are initials. GTI Mortgage tells me nothing except maybe the owners are not very creative. Hometown Lending, however, makes me feel as if the owners are friendly and approachable. Hometown Lending is a valuable name in my opinion. In fact, I just looked Hometown Lending up in the Colorado Secretary of State website and it is available. It's a great name.

I would also advise you to choose a name that describes your business concept. Names, such as KTL Services, tell me nothing about the business and cost you an opportunity to advertise to the customer. Superior Computer Services reinforces your advertising in the client's mind and informs the customer about the business. Don't waste those precious advertising dollars with a vague name.

A good name can be sold to new owners without any changes. For example, Greg does not want to own Lou's Auto Body Repair. Greg will want to change the name at some point at great expense. Unless you are world famous and a celebrity, think twice your business after yourself.

I found the name Dynamic Consulting Group for a friend
in the Secretary of State database. The previous owner had
just abandoned it. But what is important is that this name
describes my friend very well. She is dynamic and full of ideas
and energy.

Her friends thought the name was perfect for her. Friends

are great for trying out names and business ideas. They know you well and the enthusiasm of their response is a good gauge of their opinion of your new business name. Have a focus party and ask for their impressions of your proposed name.

When I am thinking of starting another business, I search for the most obvious names in the Secretary of State's database. This search gives me lots of ideas about my new business. While you are scrolling through the company names, think about how each name makes you feel. What do think the owner is like? You'll be surprised that you will often have very strong feelings just from looking at the name. This exercise will help you choose a great name for your business.

I look for the best names I can think of and many times, the best ones are taken. However, I have the rights to a number of great names just by looking every other month or so.

Don't choose a name that is almost the same as a very familiar name. I think it is in bad taste, and it looks like you are leaching off the other company's reputation. This tactic is unnecessary in my opinion. Make your own reputation and be proud of your name. That's one reason you are starting a business!

If you have any notion that you will want to eventually have a national company, check out the name at the Patent and Trademark Office at **www.Gov.com** . You will have a harder time finding a national name (called a service mark) you like that is available. If you find a good name, then you need to file a service mark application with the Patent office. There are a number of online companies that will do this for you for a very reasonable cost such as **www. MyCorporation.com** and **www.legalzoom.com**.

Mentally Walking Through A Customer Sale

I believe that whenever you are considering opening a new business, a valuable exercise is to do a **mental walk-through**. By this

I mean mentally think of all the steps you will need to do to get paid. This is like a final walk-through of a house you are thinking of buying. Getting paid is the main point of your business.

Here's a good example of a Mental Walkthrough. I recently consulted with Sherrie who wanted to start a personal fitness training business.

"I want to leave my job and work with people who sincerely want to get in shape. I have my national certification now and love helping people reach their fitness goals. My idea is that I would give lots of personal service. I would go to people's homes and bring the equipment I need. I think the convenience and my personal service would be great Value Added Benefits. My friends think it is a great idea and love working out with me," said Sherrie with much enthusiasm.

"Let's discuss this idea, Sherrie," I said. "How much will you charge clients for your services?"

"At the fitness club I go to, the trainers charge $39 an hour. I figure that going to their homes would let me charge a little more. I thought I would charge $45 an hour. Maybe they could buy a book of 10 visits for $425," she said.

"Okay, let's look at how much money you'll make from that hour. First, let's assume a friend has given you the phone number of an interested client. So the first thing is that you would call her right?" I said.

"Yes," said Sherrie.

"What would you need to talk about with this client the first time you talk?" I asked.

"Well the first thing is my workout philosophy. Most people want to know the kinds of activities you'll do with them. Then probably if they are still interested, they would want to know when I was available and how much my program costs," said

Sherrie.

"How much time do you think you would spend on that first call?" I asked.

"Probably 30 to 45 minutes," Sherrie said.

"Do you think they would commit to hiring you with this phone call?" I asked.

"A few maybe but usually people want to think about it before making an appointment," she said.

"So another call would be needed right? Maybe another thirty minutes on the phone?" I said.

"Probably because we would need to determine what day and time we would meet," Sherrie said.

"Okay, then you need to load your car with equipment and drive to the client's house and unload, right? How long will that take? Do you have a specific area you are limiting your services?" I asked.

"Gee I hadn't thought about that. I guess it could be a long drive to some places. That wouldn't work very well. I have to start this while I'm working at my present job so my time is limited. I'll have to think about that. I guess I'd have to limit the driving to no more than thirty minutes each way," she said.

"Okay, let's say we have this client set for $45 an hour at a certain time and she lives thirty minutes away. How much are you making for providing an hour's worth of expert and personal service? Let's add up the time so far. Thirty minutes for the first phone call, thirty minutes for the second, drive to the client's house is another thirty minutes, one hour of training, and drive home for thirty minutes. That's 180 minutes or three hours to make $45 to start with a new client," I explained.

"That's only $15 an hour! That's not very much. I'd have to work a lot of hours to replace my salary! This is so depressing," groaned Sherrie.

"And that $15 an hour has to also cover your advertising,

health insurance, car expenses, equipment expenses, and liability insurance among other things," I exclaimed.

"I guess the trainers at the club can make more money even if they have to pay the club part of the $39 an hour they make. They can see clients one right after the other, and they don't have to move all the heavy workout equipment either," said Sherrie.

"Sometimes it is more than worth it to have a partner like a fitness club help you find clients easily, provide the receptionist to schedule your appointments, provide the equipment and, most of all, allow you to maximize your time. The club also allows members to see you training clients and leading fitness groups. People are much more apt to sign up with you if they know your style. Your advertising overhead is minimal," I explained.

"I guess starting with a fitness club would be the best way to go. I'll ask if I can get some evening and weekend hours to get started. Starting my own fitness business doesn't look like a wise idea right now," Sherrie said.

"I agree. Starting with a fitness club will give you valuable experience and training with lots of different types of people and immediate credibility. It will also allow you to conduct some paid research for your new business. Who knows you might find a niche in the fitness business that is being ignored. The franchise Curves was built by recognizing that women over 40 wanted to work out in a comfortable environment. Maybe you will discover an underserved population," I said.

It is critical to do a "walk-through" with your business idea. Making money with personal service businesses is especially difficult. Meeting customers anywhere other than your office or studio is very expensive for you in terms of time. Checking out your Value Added Benefit by walking through the sale can show you if you are giving too much benefit for too little money.

The "walk-through" also highlights why it is so important for a businesses to keep their best customers. Every time you have a return customer, you make more profit. Generally, you will spend less time and money on your return customer than a new client.

> *I can't tell you how many people have saved thousands of dollars and disappointment by using this walkthrough technique with me. You can do your own walk-through by asking a friend to pretend to buy your product or service. Start with the initial contact and go through to final delivery of the product or service including every phone call and step. Write down how much time it takes and the expenses involved for every step. You'll quickly see if your idea makes financial sense.*

> *One solution that will make you more money for a service product is to have group meetings. You can charge each person less than a personal visit but make more because of number of people in the group.*

Let's look at more ways to save money starting your business in Chapter 3. Saving on overhead means more money in your pocket.

3

It's Not How Much You Make, It's How Much You Keep

Overhead Can Be Overwhelming

Keeping your overhead low so that you pocket more money for the work you do is the essence of the 5K Business Model. You must resist the traditional business model and all the salespeople trying to sell you their surefire business product. Why? Because they will talk you into spending money that won't save you any time or improve the service you offer your clients but will ruin your overall profit.

In this chapter I will show you money-saving ideas that will trim your expenses and fatten your salary without sacrificing one ounce of quality. For example, the fixed overhead for my mortgage business is about $500 a month, and I have use of a beautiful, inexpensive office, a business phone line, a custom color logo and a motto that projects a "professional image." As a result of this low overhead, I can offer the best prices in town.

Part of the reason I became an entrepreneur was to have more freedom with my time and scheduling. Low overhead means I can go on a two-week vacation without resenting the expenses I owe whether I'm making money or not. Being tied to a business is not my idea of a good career move.

Another reason to keep your fixed overhead low is pricing. If you have flexibility in pricing your product, you will have a huge advantage over your competitors. It will give you the ability to undercut their prices while you build your company's reputation. Also, many new business owners make painful mistakes in pricing when they start out. Surprisingly, these errors usually involve under pricing not overpricing. If you have to do a few jobs at a "bargain" price, you will still make money with the 5K Business Model because you will be keeping your overhead low.

How About Earning an Extra $20,500 a Year for Free?

Let's look at two new financial planning businesses to see how overhead costs impact an entrepreneur's profit. Hard is a father of three and has been a financial planner for ten years with a large company. He is opening a traditional business like those found in most startup books. Harold wants an office in a nice building with a receptionist who will also help with secretarial duties. Projecting a professional image is important to Harold, and he feels that having a receptionist makes his little company look larger.

His friend Duncan is a father of two and has worked for a large financial planning firm for eight years. Duncan is opening his new business at the same time as Harold but he is using the 5K Business Model. Duncan will work from home, but has an office he can use to meet clients. He believes that clients are more interested in the quality of his advice than his office.

For this example, let's assume that both men are charging the same amount for their services and are equal in talent. Let's compare the monthly expenses for each business.

Monthly Costs	Harold	Duncan
Office (1 private & conference room)	$1,500	$100
Office Cleaning Service	$200	$ 0
Phone for Office	$150 (2 lines)	$58 (home 2nd line)
Dedicated Fax Line	$75	$20
DSL	$50+50 for home	$50
Receptionist/assistant	$2,000 + benefits	0
Website	$100	$100
Software Fees	$50	$50
TOTAL MONTHLY BILLS	**$4, 175**	**$370**

Start up Costs	Harold	Duncan
Office deposit	$500	$50
Software	$1,200	$1,200
Office furniture used	$2,000	$300 for home office
Phone Install	$150 (2 lines + wiring)	$50 (1 extra line)
Phone equipment	$1,200	$100
Copier laser used	$2,000	$400 (4 in 1 laser copier/fax/print-er/scanner)
ColorLaser Printer-Used	$2,000	
Corporate Identity Package	$1,000	$75
TOTAL	**$10,425**	**$2,250**

Suppose that Harold's business makes more money than Duncan's. In the first year, both are successful, but Harold makes $100,000 and Duncan makes $75,000 in fees and commissions.

Harold makes $100,000 divided by 12 months = $8,333 per month gross. Deduct the $4,125 monthly costs and Harold has a $4,158 monthly profit or about $50,000 a year.

Duncan earns $75,000 divided by 12 months = $6250 per month gross. Deduct the $378 monthly costs and Duncan has a $5,872 monthly profit or about $70,500 a year, or 30 percent more than Harold.

Duncan keeps $1,714 a month more than Harold for a total of $20,500 a year of "free" money.

Duncan made less in sales but ended up with over $20,000 more cash for doing less work!

If he made $100,000 or the same amount of money as Harold, Duncan would have $45,000 more per year for the same amount of work.

The Moral of this Story: Harold is paying $50,000 a year for his traditional office and receptionist, and Duncan is spending $4,536 a year no matter how much each makes per year. Harold also spent $8,000 more than Duncan to set up his office. Wouldn't you rather keep $45,000 a year in your pocket? Even more horrifying, Harold needs to work at least twice as hard as Duncan to earn the same amount of money.

Keeping More of the Money You Make

Let's look at the best ways to keep more of your income. Working with businesses on the Internet is the most important money-saving method I have found. The trick is to find ones that excel in customer service and offer excellent products that are lower priced and more innovative than traditional business products. I have personally used and thoroughly investigated all the services and products I recommend in this book and on my web site **www.5KBiz.com.** Let me show you how I helped Stacy save money by using specific Internet businesses.

Stacy and her husband are starting a lawn and gardening care service. Their yard is the showpiece of the neighborhood and they are constantly answering questions from friends. Stacy and Dan love gardening and feel real pride looking at a newly mowed lawn. They have clients lined up and have basic lawn care equipment and a large blue pickup truck and trailer.

For their Value Added Benefit, they will send each client a personal note on how to solve problem areas, or to compliment a beautiful lawn, and they will offer a free personal consultation. Employees will always wear blue polo shirts with their logo to project a more professional image than other companies.

The name of the company is Better Lawn Care. Stacy would like to learn landscaping and move the business toward bigger jobs. They want to be able to sell the business eventually and would like to structure it so it would be attractive to a buyer. Let's talk with Stacy about her expenses and how to keep more of the money.

Marilyn, what expenses will I have setting up my company?
The first and most important is advertising and your marketing

strategy. Finding new clients is the fundamental ongoing job for all businesses. This is such an important category that it requires an entire chapter to cover it. (See Chapter 5, Low Cost Marketing That Attracts Customers, for an in-depth discussion of this bewildering and expensive subject).

The basic expense categories used for the income tax form, Schedule C, which you will use to report your business expenses are:

- Automobile Expenses
- Bank Charges and Interest Expenses for Loans
- Office Supplies and Rent
- Equipment and Repair
- Printing and Reproduction expenses
- TAXES – Yikes! The most painful subject of all
- Telephone and Communications Expenses
- Travel and Meals

Start keeping track of all your expenses using these categories and income tax time will be less painful. Let's look at some of the expenses you will have.

Marilyn, I want to project a "professional image" so we can get business clients with large landscape needs. Won't I need a classy office with nice furniture so people will take me seriously? I want to meet my clients somewhere other than my home.

Even small offices are over $900 a month around here.If you feel you need to meet clients in an office, you can have access to a professional looking office with a receptionist for $100 a month with a mailbox and phone number.

However, with a lawn care business, I think that you would meet your clients at their property so you can discuss the contract and look at the property. Get started with your business and see how most people want to conduct business with you. Avoid making assumptions that cost money. Think seriously about whether you actually need an office.

Beside, there are less expensive ways than renting an office that are better suited to creating the professional appearance you want. For instance, I love the name of your company and the idea of a blue theme. The blue polo shirt idea is excellent and it will differentiate you from other companies. It's a neat and classy look. Best of all, it's inexpensive and highly visible advertising. It projects the image you want without an office.

Hmm, I think you are right. But how can I rent a "Professional Office" for $100 a month? How can it be only $100 a month?

There are a number of these new types of office concepts springing up around the country. Intelligent Office (www.intelligentoffice. com) is the company I use for my office in Boulder. It allows you to be a "member" for $100 a month. Look in the Yellow Pages under "Offices" or "Office Rentals" for listings in your area.

Here are nine benefits of this concept:

1. You get to rent one of their beautiful offices for a $10 an hour.
2. You get a phone number and voice mail account that saves you about $75 a month for a business line.
3. You get a locked mailbox with 24-hour access.
4. The office has a receptionist from 8 a.m. to 5:30 p.m.
5. You can use their fax and copy machines for a nominal charge.
6. They do not require a long-term lease, so if you feel you need a traditional office after you are in business for while, you can cancel the Intelligent Office contract.
7. Intelligent Office offers a receptionist to answer your phone calls. The cost is about $300 a month additional

and this makes it appear that you not only have an office but also a staff.

8. Your business will have a local physical address. Clients want to feel that you are not a fly-by-night operation.

9. You provide a feeling of security for clients. I often need clients to drop off financial documents to the office, and they feel better giving their financial papers to a receptionist who puts everything in my mailbox.

It is important to note that if you leave Intelligent Office, the phone number stays with them. If you hope to sell your business in the future, a phone number that you can keep and sell with the business has great value to most business buyers. Your buyer can take over the business quickly without sending out millions of "change of phone number" postcards.

Do people realize that it's not your own permanent office?

Some clients ask me about it because the office has no personal items and, if they know me at all, they are pretty sure that I would NEVER have an office that uncluttered. I never had anyone care whether I had a permanent office or not. Usually they are impressed with this ingenious concept. Again it's the quality of advice you give that's important not the quality of your surroundings.

What if people ask me where my office is?

Just point to your truck and say, "There it is." And laugh. They will laugh with you and you will have started a warm relationship with that client.

We will skip renting an office for now. But I'll need office supplies and computer equipment for our home office.

Imagine a typical day or week with your business. If you envision a lot of bookkeeping tasks and printing of invoices, customer bills and estimates, be sure to buy equipment that can handle those tasks easily and inexpensively. A black-and-white laser printer is a must for most 5K Businesses. A laser cartridge costs about $55, and you will get 4,000 pages from one.

I have a Hewlett Packard 3200se multifunction laser printer, copier, fax, and scanner that I bought refurbished for $300 in 2002, and it has been trouble free and cheap.

Color ink jet printers are often free or very cheap but the ink is extremely expensive. Skip buying a color laser printer unless you need one to make money like designing color signs or brochures. Printing an estimate in color will not get you business or make money for you.

If you have a computer now, just use that until you see how successful your business idea will be. If you do not have a decent computer, buy a desktop with a large capacity hard drive, fast processor and read-write CD ROM. I recently purchased a new desktop computer on Ebay for $890 that has every bell and whistle I'll need for the next couple of years. A private seller built it with excellent feedback from previous customers. However, I am very comfortable with computers and buying online. Much of my equipment is used or refurbished, and I have had no problems. You may want to consult with a computer consultant to buy the correct size system for your business.

A good tip: Computer crashes are not uncommon. If your company computer crashes, you may lose files that contain irreplaceable information. My database file of all my customers is a good example. It would take me weeks of very boring work to replace that file. To protect that file, I have an online file storage account with Go Daddy at **www.godaddy.com** .

This service allows you to store files away from your home computer. It is like an online file cabinet for your data. The service is $9.95 a year for one gigabyte of space. One gig of file storage is huge. And you can access your files from any computer in the world. I strongly recommend using this type of service for backup of your most important files. Skip the add-on backup tape drive for your computer. If your house burns down, it's gone.

Marilyn, how can I keep my car expenses to a minimum?

The short answer is that you cannot economize on this area very easily. I would encourage you to shop around for insurance. We switched to Allstate Insurance and are paying the same for two cars what we used to pay for one.

Cars are expensive. My own personal observation is that people assume they need large, new vehicles, when smaller, older vehicles that can be paid off sooner can save you a great deal of money in monthly car payments. This may not be wise from a write-off standpoint and some people rely on a car for image. However what I recall from books like the Millionaire Next Door is that often it was the millionaires that drove modest 10-year-old vehicles while their neighbors who lived paycheck to paycheck drove this year's model.

However, you can deduct car expenses if you use yours for business errands and appointments, and this softens the blow. When I am driving around town it is rare that I do not stop to get my mail, drive by the bank, or drop off a form to a client. So one car is deducted 100 percent on our income tax. By the way, your pickup truck that you use to go to jobs should be 100 percent deductible.

To easily keep track of your auto costs, like gas, repairs, etc. and other business expenses, get a separate busi-

*ness credit card for all business expenses. This will help you keep your business costs separate from personal items. I use Advanta for my credit card at **www.advanta.com**. They have outstanding customer service and quickly resolve any issues. There are other credit cards available but be sure they will resolve billing problems quickly. When you get busy with customers, you do not want to waste time on a $20 error.*

The income tax deduction for expenses helps your cash flow, but remember, even if an expense is deductible, it is not the same as free. You are still spending your money and getting only a small portion back in benefits. *If you spend $50 on a deductible expense, it will only save you about $5 to $10 in income taxes.* Don't spend more just because it is deductible.

A client I consulted with a few years ago had a thriving business and was grossing over $350,000 a year. However, Patty spent most of the money on "deductible" expenses such as lavish dinners and an office suite with designer furniture in a very exclusive office building. She drove an expensive company car. Patty worked twelve to fourteen hours a day and was very skilled.

Patty declared bankruptcy when her sales declined by twenty-five percent for six months. She failed to keep her overhead reasonable and was unable to build a financial cushion for a low sales period. She now works for her former competitor.

I guess there is no way around bank charges and loan interest charges either.

All banks charge more for business accounts than personal checking accounts. Finding a free checking account for your business is impossible without having a requirement for a $10,000 to $25,000 minimum balance. Check out local banks close to home for convenience and chose the one that has the most reasonable charges. If your business succeeds and you are busy making money, don't waste your precious time driving across town to make a deposit to save a few dollars a month.

Hopefully, you will have no loan interest charges because my advice is to avoid loans if at all possible. If your business requires expensive equipment, try to buy it used for cash rather than taking a personal loan. If you do not have the capital to start your 5K Biz, I suggest you save most of the money before starting. Much of the appeal of this type of business is the reduced stress and freedom you'll enjoy because you won't have large bills to pay. The more loan interest you pay every month, the less money you make and the less flexibility you will have in running your business.

What about using online banking? Isn't an online bank more convenient and cheaper?

Some people use online banking and they do charge less for fees. However, I enjoy having my bank down the street. I have had to ask their advice on a number of occasions and I am not comfortable mailing a large deposit with checks. It feels better to me to give those checks to a person.

However, if your business and preferences are better suited to online banking than my mortgage company, here are my suggestions. If you search for "online banking" in Google, you will get numerous bank options. See if the bank states how long it takes for a deposit to appear in your account. Where do you need to send it? Call them and note the level of customer service. Do you get to talk to real person or are you routed through all the automatic messages? Online banking has cheaper fees but make sure you will be happy with the service.

Any tips on getting more affordable phone service?

Many cities have competing phone companies now. In the Denver-Boulder area, we have Liberty Bell Telecom **www.libertybelltelecom.com** and a business line is $40 a month that includes all the add-on services such as voice mail, call waiting and forwarding, and caller ID. Including state and federal taxes, I was paying about $80 a month. Check around and see if your city has a startup telecom company. Liberty Bell is now offering DSL for $35, which saves $14 a month in my area.

Another good idea is to get two phone lines into your house and a two-line phone system. I got a Panasonic KX-TG2740 Base System with two handsets for about $100 total. This phone system is expandable with all the features you need (and some you don't) and you need only one phone jack for the whole house. Plug the base unit in the phone jack and then just place the handsets wherever you want.

This phone system got terrible reviews in **www.Amazon.com**. Panasonic's original battery was very poor and died quickly. I replaced the battery with a Radio Shack #23-965 **www.radioshack.com** for $7.95 and all the phones have worked beautifully for the last three years. Two-line phone systems can be $600 to $1,000 new so $100 is a terrific deal.

> *It's easy to find barely used equipment especially if you know the name and model you want. I found two Panasonic two-line base units on* **www.Ebay.com** *for sale. One unit was at a starting bid of $20 with three extension handsets, and the other was the base unit only for $59.99. You can get newer phone systems for lots of $$, but this one is exceptional and fit into my startup cost budget very well.*
>
> *Check out the feedback for any equipment you buy. The Amazon Books website* **www.amazon.com**

*sells almost everything now and has great customer reviews of most items. Another site for electronic computer related equipment is **www.cnet.com** . Check out any purchase thoroughly before you buy. You will save yourself money and brain damage.*

Another tip: Some of my clients have reported hearing static and even conversations from the other line when they switched to a two-line system in their home. Usually this is not the new phone system but the switch box outside your house. Call your phone company and have them check out the switch box. The equipment for the two lines may be touching and creating static.

Will we need a separate business line? Can't I use my cell phone?

I am a strong believer in having a separate line for your business. I have had the experience of calling a business and having a child answer the phone. The business does not feel legitimate to me.

If you want to sell your business someday, having a business phone number that has been used by you for years is a strong selling point. Changing your business phone number is very expensive, annoying, and time consuming for any business owner. It makes your business worth less to a buyer.

Get a business line with voice mail and caller ID. I strongly recommend caller ID. I have recovered many mumbled client numbers from caller ID and, after my initial resistance, now love the service. You can have your phone ring in your home but when you answer, be sure to turn down the TV. If you have children, let voice mail pick up your calls and return customer calls when it's quiet. Hearing children and the TV in the background probably will not land you that big client.

One business owner I know had a policy in her home that when she was on the phone, her sons would touch her shoulder when they needed her attention. If it was an emergency, they would write a note and give it to her.

Cell phones are a mixed bag in my opinion. Often it is very difficult to hear and talk because of poor reception. For short messages, they are indispensable. But I dislike having a long conversation on a cell phone. The quality is not the same as a landline. I would recommend using cell phones sparingly. Have you ever tried having an important call to someone on a cell phone when they drove through a tunnel or over a mountain? Did you decide to do business with them? I think I sound more professional on a landline.

Is there any other communication equipment I need for my business?

My final recommendation is to have a fax number. I use **www. efax.com** for all my faxes and I get many faxes each day. Efax is an ingenious system that sends your faxes to your e-mail account and costs $19.95 a month. You can look at them and print them if you need a copy, store them in your e-mail folder or just delete the messages. Efax allows you to fax documents from your computer also. Efax will give you a regular local phone number to put on your business cards. This service avoids having a separate phone line for your fax at $60 a month. Also, you will never hear the fax machine ringing in the middle of the night.

I have a Yahoo e-mail account and, for $19.95 a year, you can buy two gigabytes of storage for your e-mails and fax copies. I store appraisals in Yahoo and can e-mail them out to clients who need a copy later. That way I save on printing costs and mailing costs. I have well over 100 appraisals at 15 pages each and have barely dented the two-gigabyte storage. Most importantly, I can be any-where in the world and access my e-mail account.

It sounds like you work while you are traveling.

I have set my business up so that I can access almost every file from any remote computer. During the mortgage refinance boom in the summer of 2003, I was working fourteen-hour days. We had a trip planned to California in July and I decided to go even though I had a couple of loans in progress. I went to a Kinko's every morning for about an hour and returned e-mails and phone calls, ordered appraisals, and locked loans. July ended up being my highest gross-ing month ever. My system worked beautifully.

Actually I prefer to get mortgages completed before leaving on vacation. If a trip is unavoidable (and already paid for), I can still give my clients good service no matter where I am.

Marilyn, I don't think we can afford a logo. I talked to a few companies and they wanted over $1,000 for a "corporate im-age" package with logo and stationery design.

Have I got a deal for you! Go to the website Elance at **www.elance.com***. I paid $35 for my logo and I got it within two days. This is a site where you can get graphic artists to bid to design your logo, stationery, brochures, and artwork. I posted my request for my last logo and got twenty-five bids that ranged from $25 to $300 within three days. You get to look over the port-folio of the artist online and pick one with the artistic style you like.*

A very important factor with Elance is that you will own the design for your logo, brochures, and art-work. You can reproduce or change these materials as you wish.

You'll need a Paypal account at **www.paypal.**

com *to pay for the work. This account saves time and money and you can use it for many online companies.*

Elance has many services for 5K Businesses. I contracted with an artist to design all the artwork for a book and paid $75 per drawing. Best of all, the artwork belongs to me. I posted my request and I received 45 bids from artists around the world.

I was able to look at portfolios of their work online and read the feedback from previous clients. Having a number of artists to choose from was important to me. What if I contracted with a local designer and didn't like her work? Another advantage was that I could take my time deciding and repost the job if I wished.

What I discovered was that choosing an artist is very personal. The artist I picked was terrific. I liked his drawing style, and his feedback from former clients was extremely positive. All communication was done by e-mail and three drawings were completed in two days. It was a very positive experience for me and extremely time efficient.

Here are some guidelines about writing your bid proposal for the E-Lance artists.

It is important for you to have an idea about what you want your logo will look like. You can ask the artist for ideas but you might want to have a few ideas about the design and colors you like. The process will go quicker and you'll be happier with the results.

Next you'll want to make up a motto that describes your business and adds clarity and value to your business name. Add it below or next to your logo and it will look very professional. Boulder Mortgage Company has the motto "Your Hometown Lender," which appeals to many of my customers because they love living in Boulder. Make up a motto that will evoke a positive feeling.

In choosing a logo style, pick one that is clean and uncluttered and has only two colors. Two colors cost less to print on your business cards and still look classy. The less detail the better. Ask your most truthful friends if the logo design reflects a positive image and if it is appealing. Some logos I have seen are disasters with too much junk or are so obtuse that I can't figure out what the company does. Simple is better. You are going to look at this for a long, long time. And a clean design looks better on t-shirts and water bottles if you have advertising giveaways.

Before you choose your final logo design, see how it looks in black and white. You will want to be able to print your logo cheaply and use a black-and-white copier for routine stuff. That's why I did not get stationery designed. I just pasted the logo onto a Microsoft Word document and ran it through the copier to see how it looked. And it looked great. I don't believe I have ever lost a sale because my logo was in black and white on my stationery.

Write in your bid that you want the artist to send your logo in all file formats such as JPEG, GIF, EPS, and AI. You'll need these for printing business cards and large items. I had a 12' x 6' banner printed and they needed the EPS format to make it come out clearly. Asking for all file formats did not cost me anything extra.

Do you have a good Web site for business cards?

I use **www.vistaprint.com** for my business cards. They will help you download your new logo and you can design your own business card. I was impressed with them because they called me directly to check on an error on my card.

You might also want to pay a bit more for options that are important to you. For instance, I buy high gloss paper because my logo has blue mountains and it looks great on higher quality paper.

Another option is to add printing on the back. I see that as cheap space for advertising. The price for 1,000 cards was $70 and they look good. I believe it makes a good impression to have a nice quality business card. But $70 to $80 is the most I'll spend. One thousand cards last a long time.

Printing is *so* expensive. We want to have some color brochures showing beautiful green lawns. The local printer charges almost $1 per page so each brochure would be $2.

Color printing is expensive and if you are going to have brochures, they should be in color. If you are going to market to large businesses, you will need to have a color brochure to give them. My suggestion is to print a limited number of brochures to start. I guarantee that no matter how many times you proof your copy, you will find an error in the brochure. I have *never* had a handout or brochure that I was perfectly happy with. I had a client who forgot to put her name on her business card. No kidding.

Every brochure I have ever done has had an error or something I wished I had changed. So print a limited number of 25 to 50 to begin on an ink jet color printer or at your local printer.

You will change your business concept many times as you get more customers and they give you feedback. Tweaking your business so that it suits you and your customers is one of the most important features of the 5K Business. It is typical to start out promising an add-on service and finding out after a few months that the service is unprofitable, useless or just plain annoying to do. Your idea about a great Value Added Benefit might not appeal to customers. It feels even worse when you have boxes of color brochures explaining the service you just dropped.

> *You can have color copies of your brochure printed by a web based printing company extremely cheaply. One-sided copies are about $.20 each and two sided copies are about $.35 each* **www.docucopies.com** *and* **www.colorcopysite.com.** *Keep in mind that the vast majority of your color brochures will end up in the trash. Give them to people who seem truly interested in your service.*
>
> *Every business owner who read this section had a story about how they ordered 5,000 brochures and discovered a critical error. No customer would be impressed by the color when there is a typographical error.*
>
> *One woman said she kept the brochures in her basement for five years because she couldn't bear to throw them out. She felt like she was throwing away thousands of dollars even though she couldn't use the brochures.*

I guess you are going to tell me to skip color stationery too. It looks so nice and professional.

Skip the "stationery package" that all the printers will try to sell you. It is unnecessary in my opinion for the vast majority of small businesses. I have never bought a product because the company had nice stationery. Have you?

Be confident about your product, the Value Added Benefit, and your customer service. Your customer will buy because of you and your expertise. They want their problem solved for a reasonable price. Color stationery has never solved any customer's problem that I know of. And of course, you can always use the paste and copy method I describe on page 10 under bid guidelines to create your own classy black-and-white stationery.

If you feel you must have color stationery, use your color ink jet printer or the local copy store's color printer. Print a limited amount of 20. If you use the stationery and feel it essential to your business, then order more from a printer.

Marilyn, I am really scared of the bookkeeping and figuring out the taxes we will owe every quarter. It seems so complicated and overwhelming.

It seems complicated and overwhelming because it is! This is why I believe that hiring a good CPA is crucial to most businesses. Having a CPA on your side can be invaluable. Interview a few and find one that charges a reasonable fee and that you can talk to easily. A good CPA answers your questions with language you can understand and makes you comfortable. If you want to sell your business, having a CPA doing your income taxes means the buyer will have more confidence in the reliability of the expenses and profit.

I use QuickBooks Online at **www.intuit.com** *for my bookkeeping. This is an accounting program that is on the web. All my files are stored away from my computer so that if my office computer crashes, I have not lost all my bookkeeping files. It would take me days to recreate those files and I don't want to risk it. And I can access my books from any computer. I always have the most updated version of QuickBooks too.*

Also QuickBooks has a user's forum where you can ask questions and get answers quickly. Learning basic accounting is a task that all business owners must learn.

It costs $19.95 a month and seems to be a cost that has true value for me. My accountant can login to my company files in QuickBooks and tell me what errors I have made in my books. And I have usually made a *lot of errors. She is patient with me, however, and we manage to make it through tax season every year. She can figure my quarterly taxes quickly and accurately and give me the bad news by e-mail.*

So there **are** some services that you will spend extra money on and some you won't. How do I know which services or products I should buy for my business?

The products I spend extra money on need to save me time, money or improve my service to my customer. Each product or service must produce an added value. Also, each business will require specific expenditures that are necessary to do a great job. Often the top software for an industry is the best buy in the long run even if it is 20 percent more than the competition. The quality has to be there for me to spend more than is necessary.

You will need to decide if each product or service has added value for the customer or you. The mortgage business is heavily dependent on computers and online access, so I had my home wired for DSL rather than risk using wireless connections. If I can't get online, I am out of business. DSL allows me to serve my customers more efficiently and more reliability. Also, I hire the best computer technicians I can find because if my computers are down, I can't service my customers.

On the other hand, my stationery is not important. It will have no effect on how well I serve my customers needs.

Look at the service you are providing and ask whether the product you want to purchase is an extra or essential. A public speaker needs top quality sound equipment, but his brochures may only need to give basic information. A lawyer I know spends $75 for the binder for her estate plan. It's a very classy binder but has little to do with her service. It does not add value to the customer's experience with her.

My friend who has a successful business thinks this is nuts! She says the only way to make big money is to be big. You have to spend money to make money. She thinks I should have employees and rent space.

Traditional businesspeople would argue that having an office and an assistant means the business can produce more income and handle more business. In theory, I agree. I have seen 5K Businesses begin to outgrow this low overhead model. If you are successful with your business, there will a time that you must decide if you want to grow and develop a bigger company. A more traditional business will be valued higher by most buyers when you decide to sell.

However in starting up a company, *I believe the 5K Business is the best model for novices because it entails so much less financial risk.* Then, if down the road you do decide to become more traditional, you will have a tremendous advantage over other startups. You will have established your business and will have no loans to limit your expansion. And you will have a great reputation because of your Value Added Benefit.

Many 5K Business owners decide to stay small. The advantages of a low overhead business are compelling. My mortgage company has the capacity to be much bigger but I want more freedom and flexibility in my life. I am not interested in working more hours, renting space, and hiring employees. I do not want to go to an office every day ever again, even if I am the boss. I like having the freedom to work with a select group of customers. With a large overhead bill every month, I would have to become more like a traditional mortgage broker and charge my customers higher fees. My advertising budget would have to be far larger to support a bigger business. I would not have the flexibility I have presently with my time and scheduling so I'm staying small.

Marilyn, I have a lot of work to do to set up my business. Thanks for all the ideas and I think I'll get started with your suggestions.

The first year of your business will be exciting and challenging. You will be refining your operating systems to fit how you want to run your business. Your customers will show you the services they really want. As you change in response to their needs, you will add some services and drop others that didn't work. Much of the success in your 5K biz will be the result of experimentation. Hopefully this book will help you avoid some of that trial and terror. My website **www.5KBiz.com** has links, discussion, resources, and new information for startup 5K Businesses. Check it out.

Web Links and Money Savings Ideas

- Intelligent Office (**www.intelligentoffice.com**) and similar concepts offer a professional office with no lease obligations.
- Get an online file storage account with Go Daddy at **www.godaddy.com** for $9.95 a year.
- Check out Advanta for a good business credit card at **www.advanta.com** .
- Check out local telecom companies for deals on your business phone line.
- Use Efax for a separate fax number at **www.efax.com**. No fax machines ringing in the middle of the night.
- Use the customer reviews at **www.amazon.com** before buying any equipment.
- Log in to Elance at **www.elance.com** to get graphic artists to bid to design your logo, stationery, brochures, and artwork.
- Set up a Paypal account at **www.paypal.com** to pay for any work at Elance.
- Use **www.vistaprint.com** for your business cards.
- Check out www.docucopies.com and **www.colorcopysite.com** for color printing jobs.
- Be sure to print only 25 to 50 brochures until you are certain of your services and descriptions.
- Paste your logo onto Microsoft Word documents instead of ordering a "Stationery Package."

Check out **www.5KBiz.com** to read about other new 5K Businesses and get more ideas.

4 Recruiting and Keeping Great Customers

What are customers looking for when they call a business? Obviously they are seeking a product or a service. But what factors persuades them to buy from you as opposed to the business down the block? (1) Your ability to develop a rapport with your customers (2) Your ability to attract customers who value quality and (3) Products that are fairly priced.

Many people would say that the most important factor is price. I disagree. Price is always a consideration, and later in this chapter we will talk about how to (1) set your prices so you attract the type of clientele you want (2) brand your product or services so you can charge premium prices and (3) factor traditional pricing principles into this equation. However, instilling confidence and caring about your customers are the most important selection factors for many customers.

Attitude is Everything

Your attitude towards your work and your customers is one of your most potent sales tools. If you do not develop a rapport with your customers so that they feel valued, it won't matter how good your service or product is. Customers rarely buy from someone they don't like or trust. Or if they do, they never return. My recent visitor to a hair stylist reconfirmed this for me.

The stylist showed me to the chair while looking out the window. While I was explaining the cut I wanted, she was somewhat attentive but often glanced at the pedestrians on the sidewalk as I spoke.

She proceeded to cut my hair very rapidly. I had a hard time allowing this after it felt like she had not listened to me carefully. With barely concealed boredom and a false smile, she asked me how my day was going. I wanted to say it was fine (until she started cutting my hair in a seemingly random fashion).

A customer walked in and started looking at the high-priced hair products (with high commissions for the stylists). She rushed over and with real enthusiasm, asked if she could help. They proceeded to have a lengthy conversation about volumizers and mousse while I sat with a half cut head of hair. After selling several bottles and making $8 or so in commissions, she came back without a word.

Surprisingly, my hair cut was very good. It was a little short but still a good cut. Will I go back? Probably not.

This young woman was bored and burned out on cutting hair. She soon will lose her best customers and end up with the customers no other stylist wants. She'll start complaining about how her tips just aren't as high as last year. Changing salons will not help her business or her attitude. She will blame the cheap customers and the hair salon.

Her product was good. I got a good haircut. But the confidence and caring part was poor. She made me feel like I was intruding instead of welcoming me. It's hard to see ten or twenty people a day and act like you are happy each person came in. But it's part of your job as the sales person for your business. Fortunately, 5K owners have an advantage because the strong interest that led them to open their business gives them more enthusiasm for their job. It's still work, but they derive more enjoyment from it.

Well that's a service you might say, and of course I want someone to be interested in me if I am paying them for their time but products are different. Are they? Here's an example of how a poor attitude jeopardized a sale.

> *Suppose you are looking for a used car. You spot an ad for the model and year car that you are seeking for $500 less than the other ads. Quickly you call and agree to see the car at the seller's home.*
>
> *When you arrive, you see that the car is in great shape with low mileage. The owner greets you but looks nervous. He appears to be jumpy and speaks rapidly. He provides minimal responses to your questions.*
>
> *You take the car for a test drive and it seems perfect. The owner is pacing in the driveway as you return and pressures you to buy the car today. Do you buy the car?*

Many people would not buy the car. It feels like something is not right, and you begin to suspect that the car is stolen or damaged in some way. The car is fine, but the seller seems untrustworthy in some way. He seems to have no connection to the car and just wants to get rid of it. This example is fairly obvious but subtle clues from sellers change the dynamics of a sale.

What if this seller acted happy to see you and started volunteering information about the car's maintenance? What if he told you he is selling the car for $500 less because it's his mother's and she is moving next week and wants a quick sale? Would your attitude change? You bet it would.

How Building Rapport Creates Sales

When I started the mortgage company, I had a luxury most new owners do not have. I didn't have to make very much money to stay in business. I designed the business to have very low overhead bills each month. I live fairly simply and have enough outside income to pay my bills. I did not have to make a sale to feed my family or pay my mortgage. Certainly my financial life is easier if I am getting mortgages every month, but having a month or two with no income would not mean I was looking at disaster.

This relatively luxurious situation allowed me to experiment with my sales technique. The hard hitting, get-a-sale no matter what it takes, strategy was not my style. This "used car salesman" technique is strongly advocated by many sales gurus but it does not suit my personality.

I decided to do what felt naturally when it came to sales. I felt that most people did not want me to "sell" them a mortgage. Giving them quality information about the costs and options available is more my style. I found that my customers appreciated the extra time I took to explain the various mortgages to them. They trusted me more when I provided information and did not pressure them.

I also decided to give them my opinion about which mortgage I thought was most appropriate and explained why. They responded positively to hearing my reasoning about their best mortgage choices. I was relaxed and confident and spent as much time as they needed to talk over their options. I never pressured them to start an application with me.

I would ask them if I needed to call them at a more convenient time. What I discovered is that they would say, "Let's do the application now." Usually they were eager to get started. I realized that this positive strategy--have the client tell me they wanted to work with me worked far better than the negative technique of pressuring them to make a commitment.

Many mortgage brokers complain about the "dropout rate." This means the client has made an application with you and, after a week or so, dumps you for another mortgage company. With my system, I have had an almost zero dropout rate. The client has asked me to work with them. They do not have buyer's remorse nor do they keep calling other companies.

James calls me for a mortgage for a new home he is buying. He is married with two children and they are moving up to their dream home. He sounds very nervous.

"Hello, I'm interested in getting some interest rate quotes," said James.

"Well you have called the right place. That's what we do here," I said.

"Great," laughed James.

"How can I help you?" I asked.

"We are buying a new house in Stoneridge and need a mortgage. So I'm calling some mortgage companies to compare the rates," said James.

"Wow beautiful area. I have done a few loans over there and that is a very nice area," I exclaimed.

"Oh, yeah. Uh, we think we will like it. It's the first new house I've ever bought," said James.

"Well I think it's a good area to buy because of the park and open space being so close. And that new elementary school is gorgeous," I said.

"Oh do you think so? We liked the school too. The house is more than we thought we would spend. It's $10,000 more than I wanted to spend," said James.

"Maybe you'll feel a tiny bit better if I tell you that an extra $10,000 is only about $65 more a month if you get a thirty-year mortgage," I said.

"Wow only $65? That's great!" sighed James.

"What kind of mortgage were you interested in? A thirty-year fixed?" I asked.

"I think so. I think that's what we would want. What others would be good? I don't know much about this stuff," he asked.

"The thirty year gives you thirty years of rate protection and, if this is your "forever" house, having protection is what I would want. You could also get a 15-year fixed or an adjustable but I wouldn't recommend an adjustable. Rates have been going up," I said.

"This is our "dream house" and I'm pretty careful with my money so I think either a thirty year or fifteen year fixed," said James.

"Let me pull up some rates for you. Let's see what we have today. Rates have been drifting down all this week," I said.

I quote James some rates for a thirty year and fifteen year mortgage and tell him our closing costs. I explain each fee and who gets the money. I disclose how much I will make on the loan.

"None of the other companies told me this much information. Thanks," said James.

"If you want to give me your monthly income, I'll figure out your housing ratio. The ratio will help you decide if you're spending too much," I said.

"Oh okay. My monthly income is about $10,000. I work at IBM," he said.

"I have worked with a lot of IBM people. I guessed you were a techie. Let's see, your ratio is twenty-one percent, which is terrific. For most families, that is a very comfortable payment. You'll actually be able to live in the house <u>and</u> go out to dinner with the family once in a while. It looks very good. If you were over forty percent, I'd be a little worried but twenty-one percent is great," I said.

"Whew that's a relief," said James.

"Okay, James. Do you have any other questions for me?" I asked.

"Uh no I think I have everything," he said.

"We would love to have your business so please give us a call if you think of some more questions," I said.

"Well, uh wait. I think I'd like to go with you. How much do I need to give you to get the rate we talked about locked? Or do I need to sign anything?" he asked.

"We don't charge for locking and you don't need to sign either. We just need to fill out an application to lock a rate today. Do you have five to ten minutes now to do the application over the phone or should I call you at a more convenient time?" I asked.

"Let's do it now. I took the day off to call around for a loan," he said.

"Well, it's only 9:30 a.m. so I guess you can play hooky the rest of the day. Don't worry I won't tell your wife," I laughed.

I have wonderful customers and I enjoy working with them. We treat each other with respect. I never "spam" them or call without good reason. I never pressure them.

One of the secrets of great customer relationships is to anticipate how they are feeling. Many people are very nervous about mortgages, money and buying a new house. It's a huge event in their lives. I try to give them as much information as possible so they can feel confident that they are doing the right thing.

Getting Customers You Like to Call You

It has been interesting to me to realize that the customers I most enjoy working share the same values as I do. Virtually all of my customers have outstanding credit, are conservative with their money, rarely have much debt, and have worked very hard for years at professional jobs.

So my advertising is geared towards folks like me. It is simple but informative. It is reassuring and straightforward. I am part of a local consumer advocate's network of businesses, and I pledge to be honest with my customers. I give my customers deals that I would want. I don't do more than four or five loans a month so I can give my clients great service. My overhead is low so I can make good money and give my clients a very competitive deal. Win-win is the goal of my business strategy. It has worked well for me.

As a result, I do not have clients trying to get me to cut my fees or complaining about closing costs. This astounds many of my mortgage broker friends. I have had clients ask me if I am sure that I made enough money on their loan during the closing session.

Don't Attract Customers Who Want the Lowest Prices

Many new business owners try to offer services or products for every conceivable market. They find that they don't like certain customers and they blame the customers when the problem lies with the owner's marketing approach. After reading numerous marketing books, they try all the tricks to get any warm body to come to their stores or call them. Cutting prices to please a customer rarely works, unless your business is based on discount pricing, and as you can see in June's case, may backfire on you.

> *June called me in tears. She opened a graphic art business two years ago and has been struggling with making enough money to go full time. She is a single mom with one child and works at an art studio part time while she develops her company. June is very talented and has years of experience.*
>
> *"Marilyn, I am so discouraged. I must be doing something wrong. Maybe I'm just not cut out for having a business of my own," she sighed.*
>
> *"What's happening?" I asked.*
>
> *"I just had a customer insult me! I am so hurt," she ex-*

claimed.

"Why did he insult you? What did he say?" I asked.

"I was doing a new brochure for him. He said the brochure wasn't that good but he would take it if I knocked another ten percent off the price. I already was giving him a deal! What a jerk!" she wailed.

"What do you mean by 'giving him a deal'? I asked.

"Well he was waffling around about hiring me so I cut my price so he would hire me. But now I wish I never started with him," she said.

"I thought we talked about giving customers 'a deal'. There's a real good reason not to do that, you know," I sighed.

"Okay, okay I know but I was feeling desperate. No one called me that day. I thought I would have a steadier income by now," she said.

"Well when you give someone a deal after they have pressured you, they think you can be bullied. And some jerks try to take advantage of that. Your prices are very competitive for this area, remember?" I said.

"He just doesn't have any respect for me. What should I do now?" she asked.

"Tell him 'no' nicely but firmly and say that you will keep the brochure on file for ninety days if he's interested. Then say goodbye. And don't whine," I said.

"What about all my work? Oh never mind I already know what you're going to say," she said.

"Don't let him push you around. You do beautiful, quality work. If he wants some changes, you'll be happy to do them. Otherwise he can start over with someone else. Enough is enough," I said.

"I'll tell him. Will you help me figure out some more marketing to do so I won't do this again?" she asked.

"Sure let's get together for coffee and figure out some new strategies," I said.

If you always advertise 'Sale! Sale!' and you get customers who try to get you to cut your prices even lower; you might want to rethink your "Sale" strategy. If your advertising stresses big discounts and "low, low prices," you will attract people who want to pay the lowest possible price. Do not complain when they try to get an even lower price. And then if you need to raise your prices, you will have a hard time keeping that customer base.

Also, examine your motives in discounting your products. If you are truly trying to become a Wal Mart type store, that is your business is based on discount pricing, then the "Sale" advertising strategy is appropriate. In that case, you will attract consumers whose main consideration is price. Be sure you enjoy that type of person before entering that arena. Work for a competitor for a year and get more experience with different types of customers. Open your business when you feel you can do a good job with eighty to eighty-five percent of the people who walk in the door

Many discount businesses have flourished using the lowest price strategy. However, you will need to be extremely vigilant about your overhead costs. Miscalculations of the cost of your product and creeping overhead can quickly doom your business. Also you will need to constantly monitor your competition to check how they are pricing their product. When your competitor cuts or raises their prices, you will need to react accordingly.

Price With Confidence

If you are not in a discount business, but are lowering your services or product because you lack confidence in yourself or your ability, you need to gain some confidence and/or experience before opening your business. Hoping that you will be a success because people will expect less of you due to your low price is a losing business plan as Norm discovered.

People never expect less just because they received a lower price. They expect to get the same level of service from you as they would from a higher price company. You will not get a better evaluation from your clients because of your lower price.

Norm is a retired machinist and loves working with wood. Since he and his wife could use some extra money, he started a business specializing in building backyard decks. He had a small ad in the local paper under "Local Contractors". His ad stressed his low prices. There were several competitors in the area and Norm felt their prices were very high. He thought that he could build a deck for $1 a square foot less than his competitors.

When he went to bid the first job, he realized that the homeowner expected him to use the same materials as his competitors. Norm planned on using nails, not brass screws, and doing simple decks designs. His customers wanted more elaborate deck configurations. His ad specified the type of wood he would use, but the homeowners wanted him to use the best wood. When he pointed out the cost differences, the homeowners were disappointed in his price quotes. Often they didn't hire him.

Norm decided to price his decks the same as his competitors and use the same quality materials. He added an extra design service and personal attention as his Value Added Benefit. He realized that he was trying to get business by being the cheapest instead of being confident in his craftsmanship. He was happier and so were his customers.

Price Your Product Fairly

I am a believer in valuing your product or services with a fair price and sticking to it. If you can offer a lower price and still make enough money to meet your income goals, you might want to give your best customers a "sale" price every once in a while. An unanticipated discount for being a great customer is a wonderful surprise.

If you have a good steady business for most of the year but typically have a slow time, having a limited "sale" is a good strategy to keep your cash flow more even. Don't do this all year. If your business isn't steady for most of the year, you need to examine your advertising strategy and overall business plans.

I have found that many customers want good service and reliability first and then a good price. These are the customers that I want to call me. My advertisements reflect that desire. I advertise in the local paper and on the Web site primarily. I do not stress low prices or low rates. All my ads stress the fact that I provide information and reliability. My advertising copy on the Web stresses fair prices and outstanding customer service. I attract customers who value these traits. They understand that a business has to make money and are willing to pay a fair price for the benefit of my expertise.

Adding Panache and Personality

Pricing your product or services is critical. Price your product or service too low and you will not make enough money to stay in business. (This is called a hobby). Price your product too high and you will not have enough customers to stay in business. Your final price is dependent on many factors (see the next section on "Traditional Pricing Factors"), and most of them are not under your control. You can, however, influence your customer to pay higher prices for your service or product if you build a reputation for producing exceptional quality, one-of-a-kind products or often exceptional customer service other companies are not fulfilling.

That's how a company gets clients to pay huge amounts for items like a purse or shoes. For instance, take Coach handbags, my personal favorite. Coach bags are made from the highest quality leather with superb craftsmanship. They will last a lifetime and the company will fix any problems for free for the life of the bag, Coach has built a sterling reputation and charges a premium for their assurance that they will always support their products. They created a brand and the implied value of the brand adds lots of cash to their bottom line. There are many finely made purses in the world that cost far less money than a Coach purse, but those bags do not carry the Coach brand and cache or have its customer loyalty. Here's what a small crafts person learned from Coach's example.

Val has been making leather products for thirty-two years. She is a true leather craftswoman and creates outstanding leather goods such as purses, vests, and jackets. Val is concerned that she is not making enough money for the amount of time she spends creating and selling her products. We met for coffee to discuss the problem.

"I have been working so hard but I am just not making enough money after all this time in business. I'd like to have more time to create new products but I just don't have time after going to craft shows for 3 days several times a month. Craft shows are the places I can make the most money but they take a lot of time and energy," Val said.

"How have you marketed your products in the past?" I asked.

"I have always done craft shows to pay the bills. But I just don't make enough profit on each item. And stores want to make 40 percent on anything I consign to them. I can't make anything if I give them 40 percent, but it's easier to just drop off the merchandise," she said.

"How much does the leather in each purse cost you?" I asked.

"I use the finest leather and it can cost up to $70 for a

purse. I feel like I can only ask $130 for each one so I don't make much," she said.

"Val, that is just not enough profit. I can see why the business is not providing enough income for you. Didn't you tell me that you had hundreds of former customers who always returned to you for special orders and more merchandise?" I asked.

"I do have a lot of devoted clients. I have a few women who own every purse style I have made," she said.

"We need to figure out a way for you to charge $200 to $300 a purse rather than $130," I said.

"Oh I have never charged that much but a leatherworker I know does. And he only makes a limited number each year. They just fly off the shelves of the stores," she said.

"What if you created a brand like that? You have a name for your company, but you need to create a brand of collectible purses, for example, that people will be able to identify by name or number," I said.

"What do you mean by that? How would that work?" she asked.

"You could name your purses or number them so a client could differentiate between the styles. Coach has each purse numbered and, on EBay, people can search for number 176 and know which purse they are getting. It reinforces their brand name and people pay more for a brand name," I said.

"That sounds great but I don't know when I would ever have the time to develop something like that. I can barely keep up with the work now," she moaned.

"Val, we have to get some workers to do the assembling of the products you sell. You should be developing new products and building your business rather than just doing the labor. Couldn't you train someone to do more of the labor so you can create?" I asked.

"I always felt like I should do all the work to have the items truly mine but I can see that you're right. I have been spending too much time doing the easy jobs and not enough time thinking of ways to make more money. I do have a friend who can do more of the assembling and maybe I could find a few others to work on piecework. But I still don't have time to think of names and start a new line of leather purses," she said.

"Val, can you find three free hours a week in your schedule?" I asked.

"Yes I probably could," she said.

"During those five hours or three hours or whatever you can spare, work on your plan to build a brand. Block out Monday morning and just concentrate on activities to develop that brand. You have great talent and great products to sell. You need to tell people that you use the finest leather and why among other things. We have to package your products so people will see the value and connect with you. Then your business will be more profitable," I said.

"Will you help me make a list of things I should do to make my brand more valuable?" she asked.

"I sure will. Let's get started on streamlining your production first to free up your time," I said.

I also advised Val is to incorporate more of her own personality into her products. Many consumers enjoy knowing about the creator of the products they collect. I suggested Val add tags to her purses that talk about her career as an artist with stories gleaned from all her quirky and interesting customers over the years. Adding personality to a product is a great way for Val to create an unmistakable brand that turns her into a minor celebrity and her named purses into "collectables." Naming her purses will add panache and the stories will create intrigue. This unbeatable combination will allow her to raise her prices by making her product line classy and distinctive.

Another way I advise clients to personalize the presentation of their product or service is to add streaming video to their Web site that targets the quality-conscious client you want to attract. This is a short video of three to five minutes that customers can open on your Web site. You could be talking about how you make a product or be showcasing a sample. Getting people to buy is all about establishing a personal relationship, and seeing you in action will help make that relationship more real. Of course you are selling a product, but I believe that people are starved for personal contact. They enjoy reading about you and getting information from you about your product. Check out my Web site at   www.5KBiz.com for an example of what I mean. You can see videos that illustrate my workshops and this book. See if you can add a streaming video to your Web site.

Caution: Make sure your video can be opened quickly and easily. Nothing discourages a potential buyer like a Web site that doesn't work flawlessly. Use a Web site designer to help you get your video to open quickly. And check your Web site frequently (once a week or so) to make sure everything is working well.

The type of high-end clientele that Coach targets and Val would like to attract may seem like the dream customers, but be aware that there can be one major drawback.

> *If you are charging a premium price because you are offering exceptional customer service to an elite consumer, do not whine when you get very demanding clients.*

Your customers are paying a premium price and they will expect a premium product. For example this may require you to be available after hours and to do tasks not necessarily related to your product. I have known real estate agents that painted rooms, mowed lawns and trimmed hedges, and took care of pets for the weekend to please their high-end clients.

Traditional Pricing Factors

Now that you understand how to set your prices and market your product to recruit great customers, let's look at eight traditional principles that influence pricing. Here are 6 factors you should consider when pricing:

1. Supply in the local market and national market and demand for your product
2. Your overhead expenses
3. Your capacity to handle more work and your desire to do more work
4. Limiting the number of products you carry
5. Loyalty of your customers
6. Amount of money you want to make.

Let's look at factor 1 Supply and Demand. We have all heard of supply and demand and how those two affect business success. Logically speaking, when there are lots of companies offering a product, prices should go down. When there is high demand for a product, prices should go up. And conversely when there are few companies offering a product, prices go up and low demand means prices go down.

You can change this equation by offering the same product as lots of other companies but do a better job with customer service. I started my mortgage company when there were 1,277 other mortgage companies in the area. Logically speaking, the company should have failed. However, I perceived a need that was not being fulfilled by other companies.

Your experience can help you to discover a business that will fulfill a need or create a need.

Starbucks is a perfect example of a company that literally created the flavored coffee market. They use a perfect business model. They practically invented flavored coffee and have invested heavily in their brand name.

Starbucks charges a huge premium for their coffee. The price of coffee beans wholesale for a cup of coffee is one or two pennies. The price of a cup of coffee to the consumer using a coffee maker at home is .05 cents to .25 cents. The price of a cup of coffee at a local restaurant is $.75 to $1.50. The price of a cup of coffee at Starbucks is $2.00 to $5.00. Innovation and packaging can create need, demand, and high prices.

How many people do you know who love Starbucks coffee? What will be your "Starbucks product"? What will be the product you can produce for pennies and sell for dollars?

Your overhead expenses, Factor 2, should be low if you used some of the suggestions in Chapter 3. Low overhead means you have more flexibility in pricing and making a profit. You can make good money with your product if your overhead is low compared to your competitors.

Factor 3 Your capacity to handle more work and your desire to do more work

Factor 4 is very important to me. Your capacity to handle more work and your desire to do more work are important lifestyle issues. Most small business books assume you want to eventually become a large business. I never wanted a business that I had to worry about loans or paying the employee payroll every week.

My goal was to have a home-based business that made me money with flexible hours offering a service that I enjoyed. Working a ninety-hour week to build a business has never appealed to me. My desire was to have a business that paid a six-figure income for twenty hours a week work. I still have not achieved that dream but that's what I want.

If you want many customers and want to grow your business, then your prices will need to be more competitive with other businesses. If you want a limited clientele that has a special reason to choose you, you can raise your prices. You may have special knowledge that you share as part of your Value Added Benefit. Customers will pay higher prices if they feel that benefit is valuable.

Factor 4 Limiting the number of products you carry

Your new business will face many challenges. One challenge will be customers asking for additional products or services. Although traditional business wisdom says that you should expand to meet your customers' requests, I disagree. As I said earlier, find the type of customer you enjoy and the products or services you enjoy and stick with your formula. Customers will ask you for many additional services but that doesn't mean you should provide them.

Often the additional products will not be as profitable as your original idea. Many times you will be saddled with bulky inventory or doing services you don't really enjoy. Consider any new service or product very carefully for profitability. Do not add items because two or three customers have requested it. You can end up with an unfocused business that you begin to dislike and is unprofitable.

Factor 5 Loyalty of your customers

Having loyal customers is one of the satisfactions of owning a business. If you have a large customer base, you can charge more. Your customers are loyal because they believe in your business. They will be less price sensitive than a new customer because they are not shopping around. Your business is worth more to a buyer if you can show a large customer base. Be sure to keep your spread sheet with customer information accurate.

If you have a large and loyal customer base, you will not have to do as much advertising as a company without this base. Your customers will do advertising for you by telling their friends to use your services. There is no better advertising than a personal recommendation. You will save a considerable amount of money by treating your customers well.

Be careful not to take advantage of your customers. Several times I have looked for bids for renovating houses and the established companies bid very high. Often I got much more reasonable bids from newer companies. Perhaps the older companies just didn't want more work and bid high to lower the number of jobs. However, if they are charging their longtime customers these prices, they may be taking advantage of loyalty.

Factor 6 Amount of money you want to make

If you want to make a lot of money, you will need to do more advertising and keep your prices competitive unless you can establish an exclusive brand or have an innovative product. Making lots of money does not just happen. It is a mix of advertising strategy and your ability to price and sell your product. Factor 2 has a strong influence on how much money you bring home. Keeping your overhead low always increases your profits. This allows you to price your product more competitively. It is a simple formula for success.

5 Low Cost Marketing That Attracts Customers

Advertising Strategies for a 5K Business

After starting eight businesses, I believe the first question to ask when considering stating a business is "How am I going to get new customers?" New business owners become involved in all the details of getting started without seriously considering how customers are going to hear about their product. Unless your product is truly revolutionary and word of mouth will spread like wildfire, you will need a way to attract and talk with new customers.

> *My wildly successful tutoring business during gradu-*
> *ate school did not teach me a thing about attracting*
> *customers and marketing. I was offering a unique*
> *product, a simple statistics teaching model, in a highly*
> *charged atmosphere to highly motivated and desper-*
> *ate people. It was an easy sell. I, of course, thought*
> *I was simply brilliant. The next seven businesses I*
> *opened taught me otherwise.*

Many 5K businesses start out as hobbies and turn into a small business. But after you have sold your product to all your friends and their friends, what are you going to do?

If you are not selling to strangers, you have a hobby not a business.

Your business has not been tested in the real market with consumers who are also talking to your competitors. Advertising is the difference between a hobby and a business because new customers require you to refine your product and service to compete with competitors. A successful 5K business is constantly refining their practices as they learn from their customers.

WARNING! The minute your new business name appears in the public record in the local newspaper, you will be swamped with mail and calls from advertising sales people trying to make you feel insecure.

> *"You don't have a color advertisement? REALLY? I can't believe you wouldn't want your ad to look REALLY professional! And your ad is so small!" They are stunned, yes stunned, that you don't want all the products they are selling. "Don't you want your company to succeed?" they ask. You sheepishly mutter, "Yes, I do want my company to succeed."*
>
> *The pressure can be enormous because you are scared. You will begin to feel like they know what you need to do to get customers to call you. They will quote lots of statistics to convince you that you NEED a huge color phone book ad. They seem like experts and you are just trying to figure this marketing stuff out. You are easy prey for them.*

You can spend tremendous amounts of money on ads in the newspaper, the phone directory, conferences and trade shows, your website, and gifts for customers. You will get mailers with lots of "ideas". All the solicitations will promise to increase your sales but none will guarantee it.

I have been swamped with giveaway catalogs. Engraved pens, magnets, water bottles, clocks, calculators, and calendars are just a few of the gifts I received free of charge within the first year of operation. I will never have to buy another calendar again in my lifetime. I get at least 12 every October imploring me to order 300 for my customers.

Every time I register a new business name with the Secretary of State, I start receiving catalogs of giveaway items. All these items look wonderful and, before you know it, you have spent your advertising budget for the year. It's a better idea to map out a plan for your marketing strategy for the year. Many times your customers couldn't give a darn about your new mug or multicolor pen. The pen is not what is important to them. My experience is that my customers do not care about my logo coffee mugs.

This chapter will help you plan a cost effective advertising strategy to create a 5K business that will generate income for you on a consistent basis. You need to find a method to determine what your business needs in the way of essential advertising and what items are just fluff that make you feel more professional and secure. Let's get started on a rational way to determine where you should spend money.

The First Advertising Question to Ask Yourself

If a customer wants to contact you, how hard would it be for them to find you? It is not uncommon for me to ask new business owners this question and have them look at me with a blank look. They don't have a Yellow Pages ad, haven't gotten a business phone line (with a free listing in the business section), use a cell phone (which has no directory), don't advertise in the newspaper, and they work out of their home. How would someone who remembered your name find you if they lost your business card?

Have a friend try to find you using typical resources such as the Yellow Pages and the Internet using only your name and specialty. If they have to do more than 2 steps, you will be not getting much new business. If you are in a very competitive business, your potential customers should find you in one step. Make it easy for new customers to find you.

Where is your typical customer located?

We would not have to ask this question before the Internet. If your customer will be from your immediate geographical area, the bulk of advertising money will be directed to local advertisements. In my case, the vast majority of my customers are living in Boulder County. My ad in the local paper drives all the other advertising I do. It is the most important advertising money I spend.

> *I had a three-month period where the only change I made to my advertising strategy was to take my small ad out of the local newspaper. I soon noticed that 100% of my customers were people who knew me personally. I was not getting one call from a new customer. After resuming my ad in the Boulder Daily Camera for 3 times a week, I quickly began receiving calls from new customers.*
>
> *If your customers are all people you know or referrals from your friends and you want more business, you will have to begin a new advertising campaign to increase your business. Your current advertising strategy is not pulling in new customers.*

In addition, most businesses today will want at least a bare bones website with your product philosophy and contact information. Many people, including myself, look up every new business on the Internet with whom they are considering before calling.

The 5K Biz Marketing Strategy

As I did research for this book, I looked at every Start Your Own Business book I could find. I never found a marketing strategy that addressed a business typical of a 5K Biz. The books discussed TV ads, radio ads, and developing a marketing campaign with your publicity agent. TV ads and publicity agents are beyond the budget of the vast majority of businesses in the United States. A radio ad that broadcasts a 30 second message during drive time 6 times a month costs about $5,000 a *month* in my area.

Literally every small business owner I talk with is confused and frustrated with how they are spending their marketing money. They have no plan and no direction. I developed a marketing plan for these businesses that helps to focus your money in your main market and helps you plan your next steps.

You have to allocate available resources to marketing. The resources you have are money and time. If you have limited money, then you must allocate more time to promoting your business. With a larger budget, you have more choices of advertising vehicles. It is important to note that even if you have a large advertising budget, throwing money indiscriminately at every possibility will often waste that money. It is far better to have a plan that you develop and follow than just send money to the most persuasive salesperson. You will end up with a mishmash of advertising and be unable to figure out which ads are actually bringing in customers.

Three Levels of Marketing from Macro to Micro

This chart shows you the typical marketing layout of time, money and the value of each strategy. The Money category shows you that if you had $200 per month to do advertising, 10% or $40 of your money would go to Macro advertising such as sponsoring a fun run. Core advertising would take the bulk of your money, 85% or

$170 a month. Micro advertising would require only $10 (5%) of your money.

Level	Time Required	Money	Value
Macro	Minimal	10%	Supports Core and Micro ads
Core	Moderate	85%	Essential
Micro	Extensive	5%	Essential

Macro Marketing

Macro marketing is advertising on a large scale to the general population. The purpose of this advertising is to get your brand name known by as many people as possible.

> *I would like everyone in Denver and Boulder to remember the name Boulder Mortgage Company. Ideally, when anyone in Denver or Boulder even thinks about a mortgage, they would automatically think of Boulder Mortgage Company. In the real world however, this automatic thinking does not happen without a huge and ongoing advertising campaign that literally saturates the area constantly.*
>
> *If you think of needing a bandage to cover a cut, how many people think of Band-Aids? When you have a cold, would you ask for a Kleenex? These marketing campaigns have managed to get large numbers of people to automatically associate their product name with a generic product. There are lots of brands of tissues and bandages but we think of them all as Kleenex and Band-Aids collectively. This is Macro Marketing a brand name at its finest.*

A 5K business needs to have the company name as prominent as possible. Getting exposure can be relatively inexpensive with a little creativity.

The rule is: The more times your company name is seen, even briefly, the more effective the rest of your advertising will be.

Examples of inexpensive Macro Marketing would be:
- Having signs on the sides and back of your car advertising your business
- A large sign over your office or warehouse facing the street
- Signs facing the highway
- Giving away water bottles at a charity event with just your name and logo on it
- Giving speeches or informational talks about general subjects at events. Be sure your logo is displayed in the handouts.
- Sponsoring an annual event like a fun run at a school
- Offering a coupon to all employees of a school district
- Having a booth at a local convention
- A one time sponsorship or event

Advantages of Macro Marketing
- Relatively inexpensive
- Requires very little planning time once set up
- You can save up the 10% allocated and spend it all at once. For example, renting a booth at a local fair may take all your Macro money for the year.

Disadvantages of Macro Marketing
- Macro Marketing does not get you new business directly in my experience. I have given speeches, sponsored road races, and stood at trade shows and Chamber of Com-

merce events, handed out logo water bottles, being very charming and have never been able to attribute one sale to those activities. So why do it? I'll say it again: The more times your company name is seen, even briefly, the more effective the rest of your advertising will be.

Macro Marketing is relatively cheap and has value other than just getting immediate business. For example you meet other business owners while you are standing around the convention center. I have gotten many great ideas from the guys in the next booth. Small business owners are a friendly, helpful bunch.

It's usually only $200 to $300 for an 8-foot wide booth at a trade show and you learn to hone your product pitch to 10 to 30 seconds. Trade shows are a great way to get a feel for what the average consumer is thinking. I have had surprisingly in depth conversations with consumers when I ask them leading questions about their mortgage experiences. I learned what I could do to make my business better from these conversations.

Core Marketing

This advertising is the backbone of your campaign. This advertising increases your business when you are starting out, maintains your income and sustains your company over the long run. This is the most expensive advertising but most effective. It is only moderately time consuming.

Your goal for Core Marketing is high visibility and consistency. Your name and logo should be seen frequently and consistently in the same venue. If you have a newspaper ad, it should be running on a regular schedule. You can have the ad run every day or every other day or even once a week but make sure it will appear consistently in the same section of the newspaper. The target population in your area will be able to count on seeing your ad. Your logo has a tremendous impact on clients in Core Marketing. They begin to recognize the shape of the logo and immediately think of your company name.

The name of your company has a strong influence on the effectiveness of core marketing activity. A friendly and familiar name has stronger staying power in a client's memory than a vague and odd name. Also the client can recall a familiar name more easily than a name that is difficult to pronounce or spell.

Examples of Core Marketing activities:
- Joint marketing ads with a power partner.
- Ad in the local newspaper on a consistent basis- daily, 3 times a week or once a week
- Listing in the Yellow Pages
- Quality website and links to other complimentary businesses
- Ongoing ad in a specialty newsletter
- Business cards
- A friendly motto and a pleasing, clear, memorable logo
- Referrals from powerful advocates such as a well-known celebrity or business owner with high credibility. Referrals have more power if the new customer can say "Oh yes I have seen his ad in the Camera. Did he do a good job for you?"
- Postcard campaign that is consistent such as every month, or third month

Advantages of Core Marketing
- Core marketing maintains your business in bad times and boosts your business in good periods.
- Good core marketing activities is often the difference between success and lingering failure.
- This marketing brings professionalism to your business with a quality ad in the newspaper.
- People will think you are a bigger business because you

have a consistent image and high visibility in the community.

- Other larger businesses notice your advertising and are more apt to see you as their equal and refer business to you more often.

Disadvantages of Core Marketing
- Expensive
- Requires some experimentation to find the right mix of advertising at the right price.

Micro Marketing

This type of marketing costs the least but has tremendous impact. It is very time intensive but very low cost. It could also be called customer service.

This marketing is very personal and highly customer focused. An owner may remember his customer's name and favorite product. You may notify a customer that a new item has come in. You remember the customer's families' names.

True sincerity is an important part of micro marketing in my opinion. We have all gotten "personalized" mail from companies that were printed with a font that looks like handwriting. We are not easily fooled. How impressed are you when you get a handwritten letter from your insurance agent explaining a policy change or recommendation? Or a call from your vet telling you that your dog is due for his shots? It feels good to be treated as if you are valuable to a business.

Examples of Micro Marketing
- Customer newsletter mailing list
- E-mail marketing letter generated from website requests. Make sure they can cancel this easily.
- Holiday cards personalized to customers and business as-

sociates
- Individual client or business gifts
- Targeted emails for specific areas of interest to a client request
- Thank you notes to clients and referrals- handwritten
- Giving referrals to other business
- Getting referrals from other businesses
- Testimonials from clients.
- Writing a "Friends and Family" letter announcing your new business and asking for their support
- Spending extra time teaching a client about your product

Advantages of Micro Marketing
- This type of personal marketing is highly valued by your customers.
- Very inexpensive and has a low skill requirement
- Can be very creative and unique if you wish

Disadvantages of Micro Marketing
- Can be extremely time consuming
- Can look insincere and phony if overdone or poorly executed

A Practical, Cost Effective Marketing Campaign

Let's look at a marketing campaign for a new 5K Business. Check out the marketing plans posted on our website at **www.5KBiz.com** for ideas. Post your marketing plan and get feedback. More in depth case studies are described in my newest book: "A Fearless Guide to Low Cost Marketing for Your 5K Biz" available at **www.5KBiz.com.**

Margie is a career counselor. She is married with 2 sons, ages 7 and 9. She worked for a large firm for 5 years but now wants to start her own career counseling business. Her primary reason for starting a new business is she would like to increase the level of personal service to her clients. She believes she can do a better job without the constraints of having to use the large company's format.

Her Value Added Benefit will be follow up sessions after her clients get their new jobs. She believes that career counseling should be for the client's entire career not just getting one new job. She has a Success Book with past clients and their testimonials.

Marilyn, I have everything in place for starting my new business except I am lost when it comes to the marketing and advertising piece. How should I get started?

Let's plan your advertising for your first six months in business. First, do you have any ideas about getting new clients?

Well, I have a number of clients I have worked with in the past who are interested in working with me if I have my own business. So I can get started with them. But I agree with you that I need a way to attract new business. I don't know where to start.

You will need to begin with several advertising strategies. First I would start with a Macro Marketing strategy and get your website set up. You can use Go Daddy for an inexpensive website that gives new clients more information about you. Go to **www.godaddy. com** and purchase their Website Tonight program. This is an easy website building program that will get you started even if you don't know anything about building a website.

I would recommend the 5 page website package for $4.95 a month. Pay for 24 months and it's only $95 for 2 years. If you find that you need more than 5 pages, you can upgrade easily to a 10 or 20 page program with Go Daddy. Go Daddy has made it easy to get a Web "presence" quickly and easily. Go Daddy will register a domain name for you with the Website Tonight for only $1.99. You can add a Shopping Cart easily if you develop some products to sell, like a book or special reports.

I prefer that clients to spend more time on the information in their website rather than worrying about building a website. Your website is a quick and convenient place to direct people who want to know more about you. It should reflect you and your values. It is one of the best and least expensive Macro Marketing strategies. Show the site to your friends and get their feedback and comments.

Okay that sounds great. I haven't gotten my domain name yet. And $95 for 2 years certainly fits my budget. What is my next step?

We need to start with some Core Marketing Strategies now. You already have a business phone number and a free listing in the Yellow Pages under Career Counselors.

Your next step is to order your business cards with your website listed along with your email address with the rest of your contact information. Use **www.vistaprint.com** and be sure to have advertising on the back of the card. You could put your philosophy, slogan, publications, or testimonials there. It's almost free space. Choose quality paper that shows off your new 2-color logo well. One thousand business cards are about $70 from your office supplies budget.

Great idea. I'll order those after I get my domain name and website address. What else should I do?

Where do you think your customers will be located? Will you get customers from your website or locally?

My customers are all from the Denver-Boulder Metro area. I don't expect to get many customers from my website. I would like to use the website as an informational forum.

It's great that you realize where your primary customer base is located. Some new business owners have unrealistic expectations of their websites and devote too much time and money to a website only to be disappointed. Sometimes the best use of a website is as an inexpensive brochure for you. How much money per month can you spend on advertising?

I have $500 a month set aside for 6 months of advertising. Hopefully after 6 months, I will have income from the business.

Since you have a limited budget, we need to get as many Core Marketing activities started as possible. Decide what local newspaper will reach your desired audience. It is important to choose a newspaper that has a large circulation. Small circulars and newspapers are cheaper but have far less readership.

Your service is specialized so a newspaper has to have a large enough circulation so that the readership will contain people who would be interested in your services. Career counseling is not a service that everyone is going to be interested in. I would look for a newspaper with a 100,000 to 200,000 circulation at the minimum so you can reach enough people that might be interested in your service.

I talked to the Denver Post but the cost is over $5,000 per month for an ad and the Boulder Daily Camera is $1,100 a month. That's too much for my budget. I panicked when I heard those prices.

Those are scary figures for a new business. Let's figure out what you need and see if we can find a solution to this common Core Marketing problem. Which paper do you think would be better for your business?

Well, most of my clients have been from Boulder and I am better known there. Is the circulation of the Boulder Daily Camera large enough for my business?

That is a question that can only be answered with experience. Unfortunately there is no easy answer to finding the best newspaper for your business. It is a matter of trial and error. My experience is that with services that people buy infrequently such as coaching or mortgages, a newspaper with less than 100,000 circulation will not be cost effective. This may not be true for all areas of the country but it has been true for my business.

But $1,100 a month is still too much for my budget. What should I do?

I can hear the panic in your voice and I bet you are thinking "My business is a failure already". Let's look at the needs of your business.

The first issue to consider is: how many times should my ad appear in a week? The newspapers want you to commit to 7 days a week. This makes their life easier and they make more money.

I have had good luck with 4 times a week with my business. I watch the ads and see many 5K Businesses with only 1 ad per week. The cost for 4 times a week is $440 a month and for once a week is about $160 a month. Could your budget handle costs like that?

What a relief! When I talked to the ad salesperson, she insisted that I needed the whole week to get results. I have $3000 budgeted for advertising so it would be 6 months before I'd start to run out of money. So the 4 days a week looks good to me. But that doesn't leave much for any other ads.

Advertising works when you have a consistent presence to the customer. Starting with one high circulation newspaper and consistently having your ad in 4 times a week for 6 months could be very effective.

You need to give your ad time to work. People need to see your ad a number of times before they are likely to call you. The more times they see your ad, the more familiar you become to them.

So let's look at your monthly budget so far:

Website, 5 pages on Go Daddy	$4.95
Advertising in the newspaper 4x week	$440.00
Total	**$444.95**

We have $50.00 a month left in your budget and I suggest you use that money to do Micro Marketing.

Micro Marketing

Friends and Family letter postage	$39.00
Monthly Grand Total	$483.95

One Time Marketing Costs

Magnetic Signs for Car	$100.00
Business Cards 1000	$70.00
Thank You Note Cards 100	$10.00
Total	**$180.00**

So you have 2 Macro Marketing activities, the website and magnetic signs and 2 Core Marketing activities which are the newspaper ad and your business cards. This is a good start. Add the Micro Marketing ideas and you have a great beginning marketing campaign

I have some great ideas for Micro Marketing that won't cost very much. They'll take a lot of my time but I have time now before I get busy with clients.

When you are starting a business is the best time to develop more intensive Micro activities. Decide the activities that you think will have long-range potential and work on those. Examples are a newsletter delivered by email, developing short speeches and talks on a variety of subjects that are ready to go, or articles on different subjects that you can quickly revise and send to a client or publication. Send a letter to all your friends and family telling them of your new company and asking for support.

Volunteer to speak before any group at any time. Call local associations and offer to speck on a general subject concerning careers. Be careful to mention your business only briefly during the talk. No one wants a 30 minute commercial.

Call the local community colleges or adult learning business like the Colorado free University and start doing career courses and vocational testing courses. Many people start with a course and are more willing to hire you if they can see how you work with clients.

Join a business leads group. These groups exist to help you get referrals from other business owners. It's cheap and effective if you get in an active group.

Develop a great Value Added Benefit and market it constantly. Follow up with potential customers and offer the Benefit without obligation if you have to.

The absolutely best Micro Marketing however, is outstanding customer service. Be sure you have anticipated your customer's needs and exceed those needs every time. Have a refund policy in place. Think about how you would handle everyday problems like re-scheduling or cancellation of an appointment. Thank you notes are a must as is basic telephone courtesy.

I like what we have done here. From the books I've read, I thought marketing plans were really complicated and very expensive. This seems workable and simple to me.

It's a good start for you. Be sure to ask your clients how they heard of you. Then you can maximize the effective Core Marketing strategies rather than adding new advertising. For example, if the Camera ad is bringing in the most clients, I would advise that you increase your newspaper ad to 7 days a week at some point.

If you want to increase your business further, the next step would be to start an ad in the Denver Post for 2 days a week as you have more money. Many businesses end up with a mishmash of advertising and have no idea if the strategies are working. Keep it simple and accountable.

Try new strategies on a low cost, trial basis only. You will get many phone calls from salespeople urging you to use their product to increase your business.

This is especially true for salespeople selling advertising. They are good at making you feel:

1. as if you don't care about your business because if you did you would spend money for their product.
2. stupid because they can't believe you don't have a big ad in the:
   a. Yellow Pages
   b. Specialized directories for doctors, lawyers or other professionals
   c. All the other "Yellow Pages". There are a lot more phone directories than just the one you generally use
   d. A custom website
   e. Internet links to Google, Yahoo and other search engines
   f. A direct mail advertising campaign
   g. About 100,000 other schemes that are "guaranteed" to get you business.

None of these salespeople will guarantee that they will get you business. Resist the temptation until you have more experience. Wait until you feel confident that you need additional advertising.

How about some tricks for writing a good ad?
Here are a few I have used that seem to be effective.

- Use quotation marks around the headline in your ad. Very effective and cheap.
- Change your headlines once a month to highlight different ideas.
- Measure the ads currently in the newspaper and make your ad an unusual size. All the ads in my newspaper are 2" x 3". I made mine 1.5" x 3". It is now often the only ad in a space rather than in a large block with other ads.
- Red is the most eye-catching color. Color is very expensive however. Be sure your budget can handle the extra cost.
- Have a logo that looks good even when in a small ad. Clean lines and simple shapes work best.
- Ask the newspaper to put you in the same section every time. If you are always in section A, customers can find you easily.

Great ideas. Any other marketing strategies I should know about?

Yes there's one more. Halo advertising is a very effective strategy and can increase your business dramatically. Halo advertising is similar to getting referrals from others. The difference is that the referral source has unusually high credibility. A referral to your business from this type of source gives you high credibility also or a "halo".

My mortgage business has been associated with a local newscaster who is a highly vocal and aggressive consumer advocate, Tom Martino. Tom has a daily radio show and is on the Channel 31 news team. He has been extremely critical of mortgage brokers and frequently features "rip off" brokers on his shows.

Being an approved business on his website has benefited my mortgage business. Having a "halo" association with Tom in a very competitive business is a tremendous marketing opportunity. Many of my customers will only call a business if it listed on his website.

Finding a halo advertising opportunity can be difficult but once you do, your marketing costs will decrease markedly. Look for high credibility individuals or businesses and see if you are able to become a preferred referral for them.

Okay, I feel ready to get started. Thanks for all the ideas and I'll let you know how I am doing.

I can't wait to hear about your success. Let's meet again in 4 months and check your progress.

Market Linking is the Key

Your goal is to establish as many links as possible to your business in the customer's mind. Here is an example of linking the marketing levels together and increasing the chance of getting a new customer.

Start with Macro Marketing

1. Your business name creates a positive or familiar feeling in the customer's mind.
2. Your motto tells more about your values and image.
3. Your logo reinforces your name and motto
4. Your sponsorship of a fun run or charity event includes your logo on the back of t-shirts or a free water bottle
5. Customers see your car around town with the name and logo on the side

Core Marketing Begins

6. An advertisement runs 4 times a week in the local paper

with name, logo, phone number, website and information in the headline.

7. You have a local office address and customers think, "Oh, I know where that is" when they are reading your newspaper ad.
8. The company name seems familiar now
9. They look at your website and it has valuable information
10. You list a referral source in your ad and on your website that is highly credible
11. Your website reinforces your values and has multiple levels of information
12. You have a local phone number
13. Customers are now certain they know someone who recommended you.
14. The new customer calls you

Micro Marketing takes over at this point.

15. You make the caller comfortable by answering the phone enthusiastically
16. You do not hurry the caller, are relaxed, and you offer useful information with no hint of obligation or impatience.
17. You are sincere with your interest in their call.
18. If you cannot help them, say so and try to direct them to a better source. Offer to call around for more information for them. They will remember your help.

Your Selling Skills take over now.

19. You can feel the customer becoming more comfortable with you and genuine rapport builds. (Hint: Smile while you are talking and it comes through to the caller)
20. You never push for a meeting or a commitment from the caller
21. You offer to send some more information or tell them where the information is located on your website.

22. You can offer them a free service. In my case, I always offer to watch interest rates for them without obligation and I don't ask their last names.

23. Offer an unusual service for free. I am happy to go over other mortgage companies offers with them and explain anything that's not clear. I tell them they are never obligated to hire me for their mortgage.

24. With every question you ask, be sure to allow them the opportunity to say "no" if they wish. Your goal is for them to make the decision to work with you. No one likes to be pressured.

25. Before they hang up, tell them your Value Added Benefit sales pitch. Be direct by saying," It's been great talking with you and here's my short sales pitch" and laugh. You have established rapport by now and they are okay listening to you promote your company.

26. Tell them you would love to do business with them and invite them to call again.

27. Remind them that you respect them too much to call or spam them but you hope they will call you again.

The Critical Skill in Business is Selling not Marketing

Marketing just gets the customer to you. Selling is the skill you must have to convert the customer into a sale.

Many of the sales strategy suggestions I advocate are contrary to the conventional wisdom about selling. Conventional wisdom and many sales books tell you to constantly pressure the customer. Pressure them to get a face-to-face appointment. Pressure them into committing with you. Pressure them into closing the sale.

I have always used a distinctly opposite strategy. I offer information freely with no pressure. My goal is to encourage the customer to tell me that they want to work with me. I ask them if they are ready to do an application or would they prefer to think it over. They are free to hang up but usually do not. I ask them if they have 10 minutes right now to answer some questions or would they prefer me to call at another more convenient time. They are free to hang up again but they do not. I do not construct a false sense of urgency to get them to commit to me.

This strategy has worked extremely well for my businesses. I prefer to have the customer tell me he wants to work with me rather than feeling pressured by me. Our relationship is more comfortable and respectful for both of us.

The other reason that I use this strategy is because I found that pressuring clients was counterproductive. Very often the client invents a reason why they cannot continue with the sale. I have done it myself when I wanted to get out of something I felt I was roped into doing. If you believe in your product and your business, high-pressure sales is unnecessary and a waste of your precious time.

Staying Small or Growing Tall

The Case for Staying Small

The 5K Business Model is designed for people who want to start small and try out the business before committing large amounts of money and resources.

> *Many small business books are geared toward entre-preneurs who want to grow their business. Much of the advice is oriented towards getting business loans, buying building, hiring employees, and becoming a high-volume company.*

The beauty of the 5K Business Model is that it a "pure" business. A potential customer calls you with a problem. You solve that problem. The customer pays you. There are no management layers between you and the customer. If the customer wants more or something different, you know right away because you are talking directly to them.

The 5K Business is a pure form of capitalism. You have an idea and decide to open a business based on that idea. You take the risk by investing money to start your little company. Customers either like your idea and buy your product or service or they don't like the idea and you go out of business. Simple and straight forward.

However if you want to grow, a 5K Business can become a large business easily. And you have one big advantage over people who started traditional businesses. You will not have loans from your startup if you follow the advice in this book.

Every successful 5K Business owner will need to decide if they want to expand to be a bigger company. Usually in your second or third year, you will have to decide if you want to continue to grow, limit the number of clients you will see, or limit the products or services you are selling.

Later on, I will talk about what you need to consider if you decide you want to expand your business. But the problem many 5K business owners face is keeping their operation small. They have found the ideal niche for their talents that offers them freedom and flexibility. Then they get a seemingly lucrative offer, but the catch is this offer will be create more stress and change the nature of their business. It can be a painful lesson to learn, but new owners must often limit the scope of their business to a manageable level to continue enjoying their work. Here's an example:

Tom immigrated to the United States from Ireland and has a delightful Irish brogue. He was a stonemason in Ireland. Tom and his wife have fixed up homes and have been able to secure their future retirement income with rental property.

Tom started a handyman business and was extremely successful. He was honest and quoted reasonable, accurate quotes for jobs. The jobs he liked doing were small projects that took one day or less to complete. His customers loved him and wanted him to do more extensive remodeling in their homes. One of his favorite customers asked Tom for a bid to remodel a bathroom and to finish an entire basement.

Tom was very flattered by this and started to bid on this large job. As he looked over the amount of work to be done, he realized that he had no desire to take on this project. It would mean several weeks at one customer's home and he would be unable to do other jobs.

Even though this large project might be more profitable than other smaller jobs, Tom decided that he wanted to continue doing small projects. He turned the customer down but recommended several contractors he knew that would do a good job.

Large remodeling projects were too stressful, would require purchasing additional tools, and hiring extra help. Tom had found the perfect business for himself and resisted changing his winning formula.

Tom realized that customers ask for more services if they like you and feel that you have done an outstanding job for them. Just because they ask for more does not mean you should agree.

As a mortgage broker, one of the most enjoyable parts of my interactions with customers is discussing their financial goals. I have been asked a number of times to look over a customer's portfolio of stocks and investments. Even though I love to talk about stocks and investments with them, I am not a financial planner. I resist the temptation.

Limit your business to what you enjoy doing and the areas in which you have expert knowledge. It is tempting to branch out when you can see another stream of revenue coming in from each customer by offering a second service. But it can easily backfire as Norm discovered.

Norm lives in Hawaii with his wife and son and owns a small printing business. Norm has wonderful customers and listens carefully to their suggestions. Often his customers commented that it would be convenient if he had a copy machine in his store.

Norm leased a self service copy machine and charged a reasonable amount for each copy. Quickly he realized that problems with the copy machine were consuming much of his time. It seemed as if the machine was constantly jammed or the copies were unreadable. Norm found he was being interrupted constantly. And to make matters worse, Norm was not making much money with the copy machine. He decided to terminate the lease early even though he had to pay a penalty.

Unless you are sure of your ability to deliver a quality product <u>and</u> make money, refer the customer to another business. Be sure to ask the customer to name you as the referral source so you'll get some referrals from that business. Your customer will appreciate getting a referral from someone they trust. And referring out jobs to other businesses can create a win-win relationship with other business owners. Tom, for instance, refers his larger jobs out to several contractors who do quality work. Tom in turns gets a constant stream of small projects from these contractors, who are only interested in larger jobs. Many small entrepreneurs set up reciprocal arrangements with each other.

To Grow or Not to Grow?

The time when you start thinking about whether to allow your business to grow larger is a pivotal point. At this point, your 5K Business Model needs to change to accommodate a larger, more demanding business. What has worked when your business was small with a home office, no employees, and minimal overhead, often will not support a business with more customers and products. Your Value Added Benefit may need to be scaled down to require less time or be changed so that an employee with less experience than you can provide it for the customer.

How can you decide if you want to grow your business? These are six factors you need to consider before growing your business:

1. Do you want to become more of a manager rather than the main worker and take a new role, which may or may not fit your personality?
2. Do you want less contact with customers? To support a larger business, you will need to hire others to do much of the work and generate profits for you. You will have less control over the kind of customer service your business offers.
3. Do you want to commit to larger monthly overhead costs? You will be committed to a lease, paying employees and increasing your advertising budget significantly to support your monthly expenses.
4. Do you want to build a business that may have more equity when you sell it? A larger business with a permanent location is more attractive to potential buyers.
5. Do you want to take more risk? Growing larger with a much higher overhead bills means you are taking on significantly more risk. You cannot decide to break your lease or advertising contracts, or stop paying your employees if you have some months with little or no business. You will be obligated to pay for any contracts, even if you have no business and end up shutting down.
6. Do you want a less flexible schedule? If you commit to a larger, more traditional business, leaving for a month for an extended vacation is generally not advisable. Frankly a larger size business means a loss of freedom.

Hiring Employees and Independent Contractors

Of these six steps, hiring employees is one of the most significant milestones in the 5K Business and a necessary step if you decide to grow bigger. It is a huge undertaking and changes your work life significantly. You will become a trainer and boss even if you hire friends or relatives "to help out." Up to this point, you have had total control over your product or service that you offer to customers. Once you hire someone to represent your little company, as Lance did in the following example, you lose control over the quality that you are presenting to your customer.

Lance is a super salesman and loves his work. He is married with four children and makes over $400,000 a year, which allows his wife to be a full time mom. He is an independent real estate broker and has worked out of his home for ten years and used a part-time office setup to meet clients. An assistant who works on a per closing basis allows Lance to compete with large agencies and still have time for his family. He has a large devoted client list.

His reputation attracted several real estate agents who wanted to work under his broker's license. Lance thought that it was time to start expanding his business into a more traditional model. He realized that a traditional real estate business would be more valuable when he wanted to retire.

He leased a large office and furnished it and hired four experienced agents under an independent contractor basis. He also hired two full-time office receptionists to do office duties and handle customers. Lance tripled his advertising budget.

Lance thought that by hiring experienced agents he would avoid training duties. He was shocked when he began getting complaints about his agents. It became apparent that these agents did not have the same work ethic or standards that

Lance did. Lance spent several weekends developing a company standards booklet and had a daylong training for his agents and staff. He outlined his expectations and standards for customer service.

The complaints diminished but Lance discovered that one agent was often able to get a very high commission percentage from some gullible clients. Lance believed that charging a reasonable commission was ethical. Since he benefited directly from a high agent commission, he was unsure what to do.

Lance figured that he would make $50,000 extra per year because of this employee.

He felt he could not direct the agent to cut his commission charge because the agent was an independent contractor. Lance feels very uncomfortable that this agent is representing his company. He is hoping the agent will leave soon.

The first year after starting the new business, Lance made $500,000 but worked double the hours of the previous year. He is primarily a manager now and misses his contact with customers. Lance is considering shutting down his agency even though he has spent more than $200,000 in overhead and costs.

Hiring additional help is a big step, but it will change your company in many ways. It may add income, but the effect of this added income may be neutralized or even overshadowed by what you incur in stress.

On the positive side, having a staff of great employees does increase the value of your business. If a buyer can step into a profitable company with long-time employees, they will pay a premium for that stability. However, if you have a constant turnover of employees that require considerable training time and expense each month, the value of your company will diminish.

Hiring Employees vs. Independent Contractors

The IRS and your state have rules you must follow when you have employees or independent contractors working for you. It is imperative that you know the difference between these two categories. Here is a very brief outline of the differences between these two workers.

- Employees can be told what time to come to work, what the job is and how to do it, have their work day planned by the boss, and must be given breaks and lunch time. You will withhold money for Federal and state taxes and you must pay unemployment and Social Security taxes. If you do not have enough work and lay off the employee, they can collect unemployment of which a percentage is charged to you.

- Independent contractors are hired by you to do a job for a certain amount of money. You do not supervise them directly or tell them how to do the job. You pay them when the job is completed if it is to your satisfaction. You do not withhold money for Federal or state taxes. They cannot collect unemployment and you do not pay Social Security taxes on their pay.

- Independent contractors are generally cheaper for the employer but you will give up some control of the employee since you cannot directly supervise them.

- Employees are more expensive but you will be able to directly supervise their worker and make work schedules.

- The IRS can impose a substantial fine if you pay your workers as independent employees but treat them as employees.

You will need to know your state's laws and IRS expectations before you make the leap and start hiring.

> *A good source for easy to understand information on this complex area is* **www.nolo.com**. *This site has books that explain legal requirements for employees in layman's language. It is vital that you learn the IRS rules about the difference between employees and independent contractors. The IRS does not accept the excuse that you didn't know the rules.*

And speaking of the IRS, you will have more requirements to report income for your employees or independent contractors. You will probably want to hire an accountant or bookkeeper to help with the quarterly reports and tax requirements for reporting. It is difficult to run your business and comply with all the state and federal tax laws. Even though I enjoy doing income tax returns and tax law, I find the quarterly reports very burdensome. It is just plain annoying to me. Be sure to ask your accountant if he or she will charge extra for the quarterly reports.

Being the Boss

The most important consideration in deciding whether to hire employees is your ability to be the "boss." This is a difficult role especially if you have always worked for someone else. Being in charge of employees for a business you own is tremendously stressful and very emotional.

You will need to think about and write down what your policies will be for employees or independent contractors before you hire anyone. I suggest you do a similar kind of walk-through that you did when you considered starting a 5K business. Except this time envision various employment scenarios that might occur and how you would handle them. Most importantly ask yourself, "Will

I enjoy handling these situations? Is being someone's boss a role I look forward to, or could grow to like? Or is it a role I really don't want to play?"

Here are some possible situations to think about and role play:

1. How will you handle employees who call in sick? What if they call in sick one day almost every week? What if this is your best employee and you can depend on him to run the business when you go on vacation?
2. What happens if the employee is late? Every day for fifteen minutes? Every day for one hour?
3. What if the employee is abrupt with your customers on the phone and doesn't change their behavior after you speak to him? He is a wonderful worker otherwise, but an essential part of the job is customer phone contact.
4. What if your top saleswoman makes more money than you do because you were too generous with the commission split when you hired her?
5. What if your top salesperson lies to your customers?
6. What other issues specific to your business regarding employment might occur and how would you handle them?

If you can role play these scenarios beforehand, you might avoid the situation Sam found himself in when he hired a friend to work in his small business.

Sam owns a small construction business and does basement, bathroom, and kitchen remodels. He is conscientious about trying to get the remodels done as quickly as possible. He realizes that families have a difficult time functioning when their kitchens are torn apart. A source of pride for him is for the job to be completed on time.

Sam hired his former college roommate, John, who is a highly skilled drywall finisher. Sam was delighted to work with him since he was a friend and skilled drywall finishers are especially hard to find in his town.

All went well until John announced that he was divorcing his wife of twelve years. John began to be late for work and often had to leave early to meet with his lawyer. In addition, John was distracted and irritable on the job.

Sam was unsure of what to do about the situation. Several jobs were lagging behind schedule because of John's absences. His customers understood, but Sam found himself becoming extremely angry with John. Several times, he and John got into loud, angry fights on the job. Sam was embarrassed that he fired John during a shouting match.

Because your profits and your family's livelihood will depend on the performance of your employees, you may find yourself getting so emotional you say or do things you regret. Good bosses must learn to take control over their emotions since many things can go wrong at the worst time.

Are you willing to supervise employees and handle more customer complaints? Many people are not comfortable being the "boss" and do not have the temperament to effectively deal with an angry customer. Do you? Ask your family and friends if they think you can handle the emotional requirements of being an effective boss.

If you are concerned about your ability to be a boss, look for some workshops that teach these skills. Call the Chamber of Commerce or Small Business Administration and ask about courses in your town.

Friends and Family as Employees

Sam's experience highlights one of the touchiest problems many 5K business owner face when they need help—hiring friends and family. It is tempting to hire your brother's son to load boxes especially when you know he needs the money for college. And you like your brother. Sometimes hiring family can be a blessing. Often it can add additional stress to your relationships with your family.

As a single mom with three children, Beth started cutting hair in her spare time to make some extra money. Beth started her business in her home in a back room. Eventually her clientele grew to the point that she was able to quit her secretary job. Her business outgrew her back room and she needed to rent a larger space.

Now Beth has a hair salon that has five chairs and a manicurist. She hired three stylists as independent contractors and charged them a monthly "chair fee." These fees more than covered her rent and expenses. Having the chair fees took much of stress out of growing her business.

To make the stylists more efficient, Beth hired her teenage niece, Terry, as a shampoo girl. Terry was enthusiastic and energetic about her new job. For several weeks, the salon hummed with efficiency and everybody's income increased.

Terry's mom, Laverne, called Beth to tell her that Terry wouldn't be able to come in next Saturday. Terry joined a club soccer team and would have away games every other week. Beth became upset since Saturday is their busiest day. Beth reminded Laverne that she told Terry that working on Saturdays was required. Laverne said to Beth, "Don't you want your niece to play soccer? She loves soccer!"

Terry told her mom that Beth "yelled" at her when she went to the salon. A family fight ensued with every sibling getting in on the discussion and offering an opinion. Thanksgiving dinner was tense and the tension continues to this day.

Hiring family members as employees can work out well. Your sister or brother can help you in ways that other employees will not. Hopefully your sibling will be vigilant and emotionally involved in promoting your business. Having a strong advocate on your side can be a tremendous blessing. But be sure to have a clear agreement about the job parameters and your expectations.

It is especially helpful to have someone to talk over problems and opportunities that arise. One of the difficulties mentioned by many 5K business owners is not having a peer group with which to discuss new ideas or problems. Having another point of view or opinion can illuminate difficulties you had not anticipated. And having a strong partnership can help develop new products and services you might not have if you were working alone.

Motivating Employees

My experience with employees and independent contractors is mixed. Employees can make you a huge amount of money and keep your monthly income steady. However, it is surprisingly difficult to have other people working for you.

- Supervising is very time consuming and, if you have new hires regularly, it can be exhausting.
- Your total focus cannot be on your customers and business.
- You will not be able to change policies as quickly.
- Employees can make your business better or ruin it.
- Your employees will not be as enthusiastic about your company as you are.

This last point is especially important for 5K business owners who have built a company based on their enthusiasm for a particular passion, hobby or interest. If you hire employees, they may lack this enthusiasm, and in too many cases, turn customers away because to them, it is just a job. They have little or no monetary or emotional investment in a business they do not own. This point was drummed home to me when I recalled my conversations with a company I once used.

I used to have an account with a credit reporting company to provide reports for my clients. Every time I called, I noticed the operator sounded very depressed. I began noticing that every employee I talked to sounded lethargic. The employees were grudgingly helpful and I felt like I was imposing every time I called. This depression appeared to be a company wide problem. I began to dread calling.

This company sends out a monthly full color newsletter. They have a section with the Employee of the Month. However, they did not ever list the employee's last name but they did have a full color picture. I found this odd and unsettling.

Didn't they trust their customers, who are all financial institutions, with knowing the last names of their employees? Did they think we were going to call and harass the Employee of the Month? Was this part of the morale problem in some way? After a while I had to close the account because I couldn't stand to call them.

Paying Others

One of the ways to make sure your employees share some of your motivation is to pay them well. I believe that paying your workers well saves you money in the long run.

Large businesses depend on hiring many workers to work and produce the product. To support the tremendous overhead associated with having a management staff and office rent, workers must be paid so that there is extra money to pay for the administrative and management costs.

To hire and train a worker is time consuming and costly. It seems to me that compensating your employees or contractors well is a good investment. Some business owners have the idea that paying your workers as little as possible saves them money. I believe this is incorrect. My workers require my involvement in their sales for weeks so having a constant turnover is a great deal of work for me.

As a result, I pay my loan officers at the top of the scale after the first six months. I do not want them leaving me to go to another mortgage company and wasting all the time I have spent with them.

Not only is it important to pay your employees well, but it's important to treat them well. Don't nitpick about trivial matters. If you can't learn to focus the big picture and let go of little things, you risk alienating your employees and eventually losing them, as this example illustrates.

I talk with other mortgage brokers over the Internet. Our community of mortgage company owners share ideas and experiences. Many times owners will be posting about their experiences with their loan officers.

One owner had a dynamite loan officer who made him a great deal of money each month. The owner had decided to start charging this loan officer for the credit reports he pulled to qualify clients. The owner was upset that that sometimes after pulling a credit report the loan didn't go through. The owner was stuck paying the cost of the credit report.

Even though this loan officer made over $4,000 a month for the company, the owner was complaining about paying an extra $80 for credit reports. I cautioned him about alienating his best loan officer but he went ahead and charged the loan officer anyway. You can guess the rest. The loan officer left and started his own mortgage company.

Paying workers well and treating them well helps keep people motivated. But the trick is hiring employees who are enthusiastic and share your vision of customer service. Finding good workers is difficult.

When I was beginning my mortgage company, I decided to hire some independent contractors as loan officers. I realized that having loan officers who would procure loans and earn a percentage of their commission would increase my income. However I was unable to find competent, experienced loan officers to work for me, so I decided to train my own staff.

I advertised and got many responses from people wanting to learn how to do mortgages. I had training sessions and trained more than 30 people. Only two of those people were able to understand the process and also had the desire and personality to be good loan officers.

The other 28 people were smart but either just did not understand the concepts behind mortgages, or they were unable to get people to commit to doing their loans with them.

This is the reason I treat my loan officers well and with respect. They represent a considerable amount of my time and effort. If your business requires extensive training, pay your good employees well and be respectful to their needs.

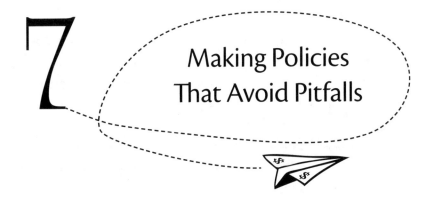

Making Policies That Avoid Pitfalls

Don't Promise More Than You Can (Or Want to) Deliver

There are numerous pitfalls along the business road. I prefer to call them opportunities but often at first glance, they look like problems. I know that sounds "Pollyanna" but it's not Pollyanna to anticipate pitfalls before you encounter them. And wish you had adopted some easy policies (which this chapter will illustrate) to avoid unnecessary headaches.

As eager owners open their first business venture, they have a tendency to promise too much to customers. They may spend too much time talking with clients, ignore potential problems when bidding, promise free services (particularly to friends and relatives), offer too large of a discount, or treat a client preferentially if they appear to be a big buyer.

One of the biggest challenges of any small business is fulfilling your promises to the customer. That can be an even greater challenge for 5K business owners. They often have an extraordinary passion and dedication to their product or service and a heightened level of information that has been learned over many years. Often the business is an extension of a life-long hobby. They can become so engrossed in imparting this knowledge, particularly if it part of their Value Added Benefit, that that it becomes the 5K owner's first order of business. It shouldn't be.

The primary objective of your business is to make money so that you can continue to stay in business. Don't let your Value Added Benefit, the extra step you are willing to do for your customer at no charge, overshadow that. It's something Brenda learned in her first months as a new entrepreneur.

Brenda is 28 and single. She quit working at a design studio to start her own 5K Business. She loved interior decorating and was a genius with color. Her business was slow to grow, but eventually she had a great client list from the outstanding referrals from happy customers.

Brenda was working sixty to eighty hours a week and not making very much money. Brenda needed to analyze her work time. After keeping track of her hours for a few weeks, Brenda realized she was giving away a lot of hours talking with clients on the phone and by promising a poorly defined Value Added Benefit.

She offered free assistance with "furniture shopping" for her Value Added Benefit. Brenda loved furniture shopping and getting just the right piece for a room. The client's definition of furniture shopping meant she would accompany the client to the showroom. This activity consumed many hours of her time.

Brenda changed her Value Added Benefit to one hour of free consultation on furniture recommendations in their home with every decorating project. This clearly defined the limit of her extra service both for herself and the client.

Secondly, Brenda limited her phone conversations with clients and began scheduling consultations for an hourly rate. She began to price her services more realistically based on the number of hours the client needed. Brenda realized that she had not taken into consideration the cost of her monthly overhead when she quoted an hourly fee.

Brenda was shocked to discover that her clients did not object to being charged hourly for her expertise. They expected to pay her for her services and valued her knowledge. Many clients paid her to accompany them to the furniture showroom. This new service almost doubled her monthly income and became an exciting part of her work life. She did not lose clients and she had a more reasonable work schedule.

As new business owners, we are often so grateful to our clients for choosing us that we do not charge enough for our services. With experience, we begin to understand why many consultants charge for telephone conversations by the minute. Consultants have only their time and expertise to sell. If our customers spend time on the phone accessing and using our expertise then we need to charge for that. Often consultants answer questions for a set amount of time, like 15 minutes, for free. At that point, you draw the line and explain your consulting fees. You would be happy to set up an appointment time for a consultation.

Be Sure That You Can Deliver

It takes experience to know what you can promise and deliver. Here are four ways to avoid promising too much.

1. Limit this extra benefit to something that you are actually able to deliver to the client.

    A manicurist I knew could offer preferred weekly appointment times to her best clients with a free pedicure every six months. But if she is swamped with manicures and barely has enough time to fit her clients into her schedule, she shouldn't offer the free pedicure. A better offer would be preferred appointment times and maybe a cup of cappuccino.

2. Begin your business with the assumption that you will be very busy in six months. This will remove the temptation to offer too much in the beginning.

3. Develop faith in your talents like Brenda did.

4. Develop faith in your ability to make money and to continue to make money.

When I finish with a mortgage, I have this sudden panic that no one will ever call me for a mortgage again. It is an irrational fear but after four years of owning a mortgage business, the thought still occurs to me. This fear has driven me to promising customers too much.

Learning from Painful Lessons

Learning is part of owning a business. It would be nice if we could avoid the pain that comes from making mistakes. But when we do make a mistakes, such as underbidding a job or tackling a job that is beyond our expertise, it is up to us to make it right. As a business person, your goal is to treat your customer fairly and take responsibility for your mistakes. Your customer should not subsidize your business education.

A former colleague, Debbie, called me about her son, Finn. Finn is 23 and recently started an above ground pool installation company. He has no employees and hires friends when he needs extra help. He accepted a job that involved moving a pool to a new location. Debbie was concerned because the job was turning out to be a nightmare for Finn and she wanted me to give him some advice.

"Marilyn, this job is killing me! I should have never agreed to move this pool," Finn exclaimed.

"What's going on, Finn? Why is this job so difficult?" I asked.

"Well, the pool is old and has wooden sides. The screws are rusted and the sections did not come apart easily. It took me twice as long to get it down as I thought it would. When I looked at it to price the job, it just didn't look that hard to take apart," he said.

"Do you have it disassembled now?" I asked.

"Yes, but here's the problem. I can't get it together again. The pieces don't fit right and I think I should have numbered each section. But I'm not even sure that numbering them would have worked," he groaned.

"It won't go together at all, or it doesn't look right?" I asked.

"It is together but I can't get it level, and I had to sort of <u>make</u> some sections fit together because the wood was warped. It didn't look warped but it is. So I jammed some of the pieces together and used some extra braces to keep them aligned. It's a mess!" Finn said.

"Will the pool be useable?" I said.

"Well that's a good question. It is so uneven that when the water is pumped in, one of the walls might give way. I'm not sure if the walls will hold water or not," he said.

"What have you told the customer?" I asked.

"Uh, well, uh I haven't told him anything. I talked him into hiring me. He didn't want to at first because he thought I was too young and inexperienced. So I'm really embarrassed that I can't get the pool installed correctly," said Finn.

"So you made a mistake. How much is the pool worth?" I asked.

"The pool is not worth anything unless he left it where it was set up. I shouldn't have taken it down and thought I could reassemble it. It was a big mistake. And he paid me $300 already. I've worked over 30 hours on this so far. I thought it would take me 10 hours. I'm losing my shirt here and the pool isn't any good," Finn said.

"So what do you think you need to do?" I asked.

"I guess I need to talk to the customer. But I don't want to. I'm dreading it. He's going to think I'm a jerk. And I feel like a jerk already," Finn groaned.

"It is going to be a very humbling conversation for you. But just show him what happened and tell him how the wood is warped. Most people understand if you have a legitimate story. He might be upset but no one else could have moved the pool either. Even if they were more experienced. Another pool installer may have known that you can't move a wooden pool. What else are you planning to do to fix this situation?" I said.

"Are you going to tell me to give his money back? After all my work? All those hours?" Finn exclaimed.

"You made a mistake. If you had told him before accepting the job that you weren't sure that the pool could be reassembled, he would have known that paying the $300 was a gamble and possibly made a different decision. Or you could offer to assemble a new pool for free or a discount," I said.

"Oh man. This was a huge lesson for me. I'll give him those options I guess. This is truly painful. I have learned a lot about wooden pools," he said.

"I think you have learned a lot about customer service and bidding on a job," I said.

Let's look at some strategies to avoid getting in this type of dilemma.

- Be honest with your customer if you are not experienced in a particular job.
- Take some time to walk around the job site or think about the proposal if you are unsure. It's okay to say that you will need to do some research and think about possible problems.
- Talk the job over with a spouse or friend. Many times explaining the work required to someone else will make the skills needed clearer.
- Be upfront with your customer ahead of time. Don't be so eager to please your customer that you fail to point out potential problems.
- Do a walk-through with your client. What if I take this apart or do this and this happens? How would you like me to handle that?
- Be realistic and don't paint worse-case scenarios, but let the owner know about any issues that could affect the project's outcomes. Learning how the owner would like them handled before they become a problem simplifies your problem solving and earns your customer's trust.

"Free" Is Expensive

We are all a bit naïve and believe the best in people particularly our friends and family members. However, setting a precedent by giving discounts and free services when you are starting a business is a pitfall that is especially fraught with trouble. Unfortunately a policy towards friends and family is usually not defined by many businesses. And therein lies a disaster waiting to happen.

Jackie was the mother of four and lived in a small town. She attended night school for her bachelor's degree and then worked for an accounting firm while she studied for her CPA designation. Since she wanted to have flexible hours while raising her children, she opened an income tax preparation business in town rather than continuing to commute to the city.

During the first year, business was a little slow. A long-time friend, Arlene, would drop by the office several times a week to talk and share coffee. Frankly Jackie was happy to have a visitor since she was a little lonely. The visits began to last an hour or so as Arlene was going through a divorce and needed Jackie's support and advice. Money was tight for her friend so Jackie offered to do Arlene's income tax return for free. Arlene was delighted and brought in her tax information the next day. She brought Jackie a beautiful bouquet of flowers in appreciation.

When she opened Arlene's tax folder, Jackie was startled to see that Arlene had an unusually complex tax return. She had income from a family trust and a small rental house, and her husband owned a part-time business that was an S corporation. Jackie realized that Arlene's tax return was going to take many hours to complete and would require numerous requests for more information. Jackie would have earned a very good commission if Arlene was paying her.

Jackie was very uncomfortable and depressed with the situation. She felt she could not tell Arlene that she couldn't do her return for free. And she felt very resentful of Arlene for not telling her that she had all these sources of income. Jackie realized that Arlene made much more money per year than her family.

Jackie did the return and didn't charge Arlene. She resented every minute she spent on it and her attitude spilled over to their relationship. To make matters worse, Jackie began to get a lot more customers as the April 15th tax deadline drew near. Jackie had to finish Arlene's tax return over a weekend and vowed to never do another free job again.

Repeat after me: Never work for free even if it's your best friend. Particularly if it is your best friend!

There are times that it seems like the charitable thing to do. However, unless you are a much nicer person than me, you will resent the time you spend on it.

I have observed that two people will use the same language to describe their financial situation but their situations are radically different. One friend has said to me, "I don't have any money" when I know she has $40,000 in the bank. Another friend has complained about not having any money and she is being evicted. Which friend are you going to give the free service to? They are both sincere about how "poor" they feel. Rather than making value judgments about who actually deserves your free services, just don't do "free." Save yourself the trouble.

Don't Do "Free"--Your Relationships Are At Risk!

It is paradoxical but often when you do a free service for someone, they almost seem to resent you for it. They will be dismissive and minimize the amount of work you are doing. You are trying to be altruistic and you have good intentions. But your friend is acting very cool. Why is this more often true than not?

My experience with giving away my services is that it diminishes my relationship with the receiver. The other person is put in a position to accept your largess usually when they cannot reciprocate equally. You now have an unequal relationship with your best friend or family member. They feel diminished in your eyes. You are more powerful than they are. The friend feels beholden to you and the playing field is no longer equal. They are in a lower status now.

And unequal relationships are not healthy or fun.

The free service highlights the fact that your friend or family member can't afford your services, does not have the same skills or is in some way less advantaged. To save their own sense of self, often they will try to be very blasé about what you have done for them. And you will be incredibly annoyed when they display that behavior. Giving away your services is a "lose-lose" situation, and giving discounts or selling at cost to friends and family is no different.

Discounts Can Be Dangerous

I have had new business owners give their families their merchandise or product at cost. Or give a generous "Friends and Family" discount. Many times new owners are startled to realize that their friends and family are their main customers. Your "warm" circle of friends and family can easily become your most profitable customers because you did not have to spend money to advertise for their business. Often they are the people that are still buying your product or service during slow business months. If you give them a discount, you will be working for free and that does not pay the bills.

> *Remember you are setting a precedent when you offer a discount or free services, and the rest of your family members and friends will expect the same treatment. When you get tired of giving this free service and stop giving the freebies, the result is often resentment.*

Problems with discounts:

- Limiting the discount to just a few family members. How do you draw the line? Are you willing to give the discount to your rich brother-in-law?

- Limiting the discount to your best friends. Are you going to tell someone that he is not a good enough friend to get the discount?
- Can you limit how many times the friend gets the discount? What if you have a product that someone buys every week or month? Do they get a discount forever?
- It's very uncomfortable to take a discount away when you realize you have made a mistake, especially if your business is successful.

Start with a "no-discount" policy and stick to it.

- Don't do anything for free unless there is a definite benefit for your business such as a barter arrangement. For example, a friend will fix your furnace if you give him fence posts at cost and you are both clear about this one-time arrangement.
- Do not do something just for "good will" because you think the person or organization will like you better and maybe send you some business.
- Put it in writing. Samuel Goldwyn said, "A verbal agreement is not worth the paper it's written on." And he was right!
- Offer a free fifteen-minute consultation but be clear that after those fifteen minutes, further conversation is on the clock.
- Do a quid pro quo arrangement. If you do something for them, they do something for you. If it is an organization, you could ask for a one time use of their mailing list, three letters of recommendations, or a free ad in their newsletter (be sure to negotiate a big ad! You are worth it!).

Getting Paid

Asking to be paid for your services can be uncomfortable, even more so if it is a friend, family member or even an acquaintance. Many people who start a business have never asked someone to pay them. They were accustomed to always being paid on time. So it is a shock when they realize that some people routinely avoid paying their bills. And they are not embarrassed by owing you money. Even when they see you frequently.

Personally I could not show my face in public if I owed someone money. I learned quickly that there are people who do not have that sense of shame. They often owe money to many people and have rationalized not paying them. Chances are you are not the first person they have "stiffed." I used to be reticent about asking them for the money they owed me, but I learned that they are not embarrassed at all. This is not the first time someone has demanded money from them. Face it: some people do not pay their bills and if you are not assertive, you will not be paid.

As a new business owner, I was eager to do as many mortgages as possible. When an acquaintance asked me to help her refinance her home, I was happy to begin her application. As a requirement of the mortgage, an appraisal was required. This acquaintance said she did not have the money to pay for the appraisal so I offered to pay for it with reimbursement at closing.

You know the end of this story, don't you? The mortgage did not go through and she refused to pay me the $300 for the appraisal. I sent a letter requesting payment but it was ignored. After several very uncomfortable phone calls, I gave up. But I haven't forgotten. When I see this person, she is always pleasant to me but has never paid me.

Do not assume other people will act with integrity just because you do. You cannot shame the shameless.

You will encounter people who will try to convince you to work for less. Or will try to pay you less than you agreed on. Some of these people are very good at making you feel like you did not deserve to be paid because you did a bad job, were late one day, or any number of minor complaints. It can be a difficult experience.

Practice asking for money that you are owed in a calm and unemotional way. Talking directly with the person is the best way. Here's an example.

John is a plumber and he helped out a friend of a friend by going to his house late one night to stop a water leak.

"Hello Bill. I'm calling to find out when I can expect the $200 you owe me for the plumbing job," said John.

"Well John I just don't have the money this month to pay you. Sorry," said Bill.

"I need to be paid for the work I did for you," asked John.

"I was hoping to pay you next month. It's really tight this month," said Bill.

"I need you to pay something this month," said John.

"Okay John. I could send you $25," said Bill.

"I need at least $100. That would pay half of what you owe me. Remember I came over late at night and didn't charge you an extra fee for that," said John.

"I could send you $75 I guess. I'll put a check in the mail," said Bill.

"I'll be in your area today so I'll stop by and pick up the check. Your bill is overdue by 90 days already so I need the money today. I can check on the seal in that pipe while I'm there," said John.

"Uh, okay I guess that's okay," said Bill.
"How about 1 o'clock?" said John.

The trick to getting bills paid by a client is to use the Broken Record strategy. Ask for the money and *then stop talking*. Let them answer. Repeat your request. Let them answer. Compromise if you have to, by asking for partial payment with subsequent payments to follow, but always ask for more money than they suggest. It's a hard situation to be in.

If a slow paying client calls you again for a job, ask for a 50% deposit up front. And don't be shy about telling them that it was difficult to collect money from them for the previous job. Or refuse the job. Weed out bad customers. Doing work that you don't get paid for is not part of owning a business.

Keeping Your Passion: Sharpen Your Ax

One of the pitfalls of starting a business providing a product or service that you are passionate about is burnout. Burnout can be a big problem for entrepreneurs since they must provide all the momentum to keep their business going. If you let your motivation slip, your business will suffer. Too often it takes a caring friend to point this out.

A man begins a firewood business. The first day he chops six cords of wood. The second day he chops five cords of wood. The third day he chops three cords of wood. On the fourth day, he is talking to a friend and he says "Gee, I was chopping six cords of wood a day and now I can only do three cords. I wish I could chop six cords every day." The friend replies "How often do you sharpen your ax?" The man says, "Oh, I don't have time to sharpen my ax. I need to get all this wood chopped."

How do you know if you're burning out? If you agree with the majority of these statements, particularly during your peak energy times, you are very likely a candidate.

- You groan if your business phone rings one more time
- You don't want to read one more article that deals with your product
- You no longer keep up with the accounting or filing
- You have fleeting thoughts about shutting down
- You are beginning to wonder why you started this business in the first place
- You are not enjoying talking with customers like you used to
- Customers are starting to annoy you

It is possible that it is time to do something new. You may have gotten all you can from this business. Certainly I have switched my focus a number of times as you'll read in Chapter 9. I shut down seven businesses after I felt I had gotten as much knowledge as I could from them. I was eager to go onto another and more profitable business.

Before you shut your doors try a few strategies first. Perhaps you have not taken care of yourself or given yourself time or activities that would recharge your enthusiasm. Take a couple of days off and sharpen your ax.

Recharging Activities

Many 5K business owners work alone much of the time. They often quit office jobs where they were in contact with co-workers every day, all day. Even though many 5K owners cite the office politics and interaction as a primary reason for wanting to leave, contact with other people is important. That contact is stimulating even if it is sometimes irritating to you.

Working alone is not just lonely; it can sap your energy. Sharing trivial information or talking over a work problem is revitalizing. Getting a fresh view and interrupting your usual train of thought often brings new ideas to solve problems.

If you are working in your home, you will need to get out of the house. I found that I needed to go out to dinner with friends especially when I was busy with lots of mortgages. I felt house bound and stagnant. I just could not face cooking dinner. I needed some fresh air and a different environment with another person. Doing errands alone during the day just did not give me the break I needed.

Ways to Sharpen Your Ax

- Join a business group that meets weekly for breakfast or lunch
- Start a coffee group with some friends
- Join a trade group that meets monthly so you can talk to other business people in the same field
- Go for a walk around the neighborhood every morning or afternoon
- Have a regular hike or activity that you schedule with a friend
- Schedule a lunch or two a week with a friend
- Join an exercise class
- Take a nap
- Engage in a daily relaxation exercise, like yoga, chi gong, or meditation
- Take a 4 day vacation to a nearby resort
- Develop interest in another passion if your business is now your former hobby.
- Take a class in that area in a new interest
- Write a book or article about your business
- Add another service to your business that would be fun for you

Suppose you do all these activities and are still feeling burned out. You may decide that you have done all you can do with this business and that you are ready to move on. The next chapter, "Handling Your Emotional Investment" may help you manage your feelings and conflicts about owning a business.

8 Handling Your Emotional Investment

It was surprising to me how emotional starting a business was. I found myself buffeted by emotions every day. It was easy to feel overwhelmed by all the tasks I needed to complete. I was learning many new skills, dealing with suppliers and trying to get all my computer programs working correctly. It was not about doing the work. Doing the work was the easy part. Dealing with my emotions while doing the work was the hard part.

That's hardly surprising. Starting a new business is exciting and stimulating, but it is also challenging and frightening. It is a literal cornucopia of emotions. Few people realize that when you start a business you are making an emotional investment as well as a financial investment. And putting your ego and self-confidence on the line, as well as your cash. In fact with a 5K business, your emotional investment may feel considerably weightier than your startup capital. Many people focus on the nuts and bolts—getting all details the business up and running while they suppress all the feelings running amok in their heads. So how do you lower your emotional risk? By cultivating your resilience.

Resiliency

Your level of resiliency is crucial to your success and, more importantly, your personal comfort with being self employed. Highly resilient people have the following personality traits:

- Curiosity. Resilient people ask lots of questions and enjoy wondering "What if I did…"
- Learn from experiences. Unexpected results are quickly absorbed and the new knowledge is assimilated.
- Adapt rapidly. They are very flexible and are always willing to try a new plan if the original plan is not working
- Solid self esteem and confidence. They are able to receive compliments and criticism.
- Good friendships and relationships. Highly resilient people have strong friendships and families. They have trusted confidants to talk over problems and successes.
- Express feelings honestly and compartmentalize them when necessary. They can express anger, love and disappointment, but they also can suppress feelings if it is more appropriate.
- Highly optimistic. They are positive thinkers and have a high tolerance for ambiguity.
- Empathy for others. They are sensitive to the needs and feeling of others.
- Intuitive and creative. They use information from many different sources to come to new and innovative conclusions.
- Deep sense of self. They are ethical and true to their convictions.
- Learn life lessons in a positive manner. They use the hard lessons from life in a positive manner and so not feel victimized. They convert misfortune into good luck and gain strength from adversity.

As you can see from this list, highly resilient people have an armory of emotional weapons to defend against the difficult times that come with starting any new business. Most of us have some of these traits and are working on others. Here are some proven strategies I've used that will help you develop your resilience.

Letting Go of Hurt

When you've done a simply spectacular job for a client, and the client (often) does not acknowledge it, it's easy to feel hurt. But I learned that in business, resentment is not productive.

One of the first mortgages I did as a new owner was for a client who had many problems with his credit. I spent literally hours on the phone getting errors on his credit report straightened out. His credit score zoomed as a result and I was able to get him a prime rate loan which saved him thousands of dollars over a year. I was very proud of myself.

At the closing however, he was dismissive about the level of service I had given him. It was very hurtful to have my hours of free work ignored. It was difficult for me to be pleasant with him since he appeared to devalue my work. I realized that I believed he owed me something for helping him. I wanted praise and I wasn't going to get it.

I had to face the fact that I offered to do this work. He never asked for it and I never asked to be paid for the credit repair. I learned that unless I was going to do an extra job with no expectation of reward, I shouldn't offer additional services. I changed my attitude and now will either do the job freely, or charge an extra fee so I am compensated for my expertise and time.

Feeling hurt that your work was not acknowledged is understandable but deciding to never offer an extra service again is not the best response. Make the lesson positive and decide your parameters for extra work. You have been given a valuable lesson in business and all it cost you is your time (and some hurt feelings). Use the emotion you felt as motivation to limit your services and make a price list for the extras.

Forgive Yourself

You will make errors in judgment when you start out. You will underestimate, overestimate and forget to estimate jobs. You will forget appointments or show up at the wrong time or day at the wrong address. Or show up with the wrong equipment. It is part of the first year of business and we have all done it.

The crucial part of making errors is your response to it. Can you forgive yourself for making mistakes? Can you learn the lesson that mistake taught you and move on emotionally as Janet did?

> *Janet is a therapist who specializes in treating clients with post traumatic stress syndrome. Her clients have been through terrible ordeals and are often very fragile emotionally.*
>
> *I was helping Janet with a mortgage for her new house and called to give her a mortgage update and she answered almost in tears. She had forgotten to meet a client at her office. The client waited for over thirty minutes. Janet was humiliated and very upset that she had added to this client's stress.*
>
> *Janet's response to the client was a sincere apology and the offer of a free appointment to compensate the client. The client was grateful for the concern and free appointment and continued therapy with Janet.*

Mistakes happen and sometimes they are totally your fault because you weren't paying full attention. Forgive yourself and move on. The best response is to do what Janet did: Apologize sincerely and offer a benefit.

Let's see how Jack handled a bid from a big customer.

My friend, Jack, had a landscaping business that he ran with his wife and grown sons. The first year in business, Jack had a golden opportunity to install a very large sprinkler system and landscaping in an expensive new home. Jack was thrilled with the job since work was getting slow. His mortgage was due along with a car payment, and he was getting worried about how he was going to pay the bills.

Jack spent many hours on the estimate for the job and felt like he had covered everything. The homeowner accepted the bid and Jack bought all the materials and got to work. As he was running his trencher to lay the sprinkler pipe, Jack hit rock and nicked the blade on the trencher. Digging down, Jack realized that the whole yard had rocks below the surface and that most of the rock would need to be removed and hauled away. He quickly realized that the trenches would have to be dug by hand or he would have to rent heavier equipment at great expense.

The homeowner refused to pay more for the job because he said he told Jack that the yard had a lot of rocks when they built the house. Jack realized that he should have asked more questions about that comment before bidding on the job. The homeowner hired another company with heavier equipment to do the landscaping. Jack had to take money out of savings to cover his bills that month.

Jack had a difficult time forgiving himself for that error. He was extra careful with bidding after that. His wife was supportive and they developed a more detailed bidding form so this situation would not happen again.

The positive response Jack had to making a mistake was to develop a better system. A poor response would have been to blame the homeowner, get angry, and threaten to sue for the repair of the trenching machine, or quit the business.

For example, I was opposed to caller ID until I forgot (several times) to write down the phone number of the client. I realized that having their phone numbers stored on my phone for a few days was a handy system to compensate for my neglect. I often get so involved in talking with a client that I forget to do the essential things like get their phone numbers so having Caller ID is a great backup system for me.

Develop systems that allow you to use your strengths to their best advantage. And this applies to any employees you may hire.

A friend of mine had an incredible salesman, Peter, who sold twice as much as anyone else in the company. Peter, however, was terrible at paperwork so my friend was continually on him to get his paperwork finished. I suggested that perhaps having one of the administrative assistants do his paperwork would be a very profitable idea.

My friend was worried about what the other salespeople would say. I said, "Tell them that when they sell as much as Peter, you'll get someone to do their paperwork too!" Someone who is great at selling and makes money for you should be out selling not filling out routine forms.

Another common scenario that requires forgiveness is when you decide to give a client a great deal. You have cut your usual prices and are throwing in some extra time for free. The client expresses his appreciation for the good price. As you are doing the job, however, you begin to feel that the expression of appreciation is not quite enough. And as the job progresses you become positive that the appreciation is not nearly enough for cutting your profit. By the end of the work, you are secretly seething and don't ever want to work with this client again. You are blaming the client for your mistake. You offered the price and he took it.

Now you need to forgive yourself for under pricing your work and forgive the client for accepting. The important lesson you've learned is that you do not like working for less so don't do it anymore. You value your work and want others to value it too. Do not give great deals if they are one sided and favor the client at your expense.

Bounce Back

Being able to recover after a bad experience is critical to your success in business and in life. Feeling bad about an incredibly stupid mistake is okay for a short time. You messed up with a client and are feeling bad. But, you will need to put that feeling aside when you visit or talk to your next client.

Do not bring that hangdog, "I'm no good and I just screwed up big time" attitude to your next appointment. The new client doesn't know about the mistake and does not care. *Do not tell your clients about your mistakes.* This is your client, not your therapist. You reduce your credibility by not being in control of your feelings in a professional manner. Use your support network to confess your sin and to bounce back.

Compartmentalizing your feelings, when appropriate, is a positive trait and is part of the repertoire of successful people. Put those feelings of shame and inadequacy in the back of your mind while you are dealing with a new client. Successful people are able to compartmentalize their feelings when appropriate.

Act As If

Another strategy I use frequently is what I call, "Act As If." When I am in an unfamiliar or difficult situation and am not sure how to act or what to do, I ask myself, "What would a confident person do in this situation?" Then I act as if I am that person. It may sound simplistic but it works very well.

I started doing this in junior high. I watched the "popular" kids and thought about why people liked being around them. I thought that others liked them because they acted as if they were confident. It seemed like a good idea for me to act that way too. It surprised me when I found that it not only worked, but I truly became more confident and sure of myself. It turns out that if you practice acting a certain way, you are rehearsing new behavior and will learn how to act that way in reality.

Act the way you want to be, and it will become an established habit. Part of the reason this works is because other people perceive you in a different way and begin to reinforce you for acting a particular way.

Pretend to be confident when you are giving estimates or talking to a new client and eventually you will be more confident. For example, confident people stand up straight, make eye contact, shake hands firmly, wait to speak, don't interrupt others, and speak clearly.

To change your behavior, you first must be aware of the behaviors you want to acquire. Write down clearly how you want to act in a particular situation and ask your friends to help you. Role play those behaviors with them and then eventually with your clients. You'll be surprised how effective this can be.

Robin felt like she was not very effective with clients who questioned her closely about her services. She realized that she tended to start babbling, get nervous and grow defensive when a client asked lots of questions. Robin made up a list of behaviors that she wanted to learn to do in those situations.

She wanted to be calm, more humorous and easy going, answer with one or two sentences and let the client ask anything they wanted without interrupting. She put the list on her wall near the phone and looked at it when she was in those situations. She found that after a few times, she didn't even need to look at the list.

Handling Disappointment

I had a professor tell me that the measure of maturity is the ability to handle disappointment. Getting through feelings of disappointment is one of the big challenges of life. Spouses, children, siblings, and parents will all disappoint you at some time in their lives. You will disappoint them at some point in your life. Your response to those strong feelings will determine how your relationship will be with the other person.

In business, disappointment can occur for various reasons. It is particularly acute when you lose a regular client to another firm and your bills are due. You were counting on that client to give you enough work to keep you going. You are hurt and feel rejected that the client you personally liked left you after all you did for them. You begin to question why they left you. You may berate yourself further, wondering why you are in this stupid business and start thinking that you should get a regular job.

Disappointment in employees is another bruising experience. Your favorite employee calls in sick when you have a huge order to send out. Or she comes in late or just doesn't appear to care as much as she used to about getting the work done. Or you might realize one of your employees is stealing from you. You are hurt because you have tried to pay your employees well, and you thought they were honest and respected you. You feel betrayed and rejected.

Monetary problems can be particularly distressing since your business's success hinges on keeping it financially solvent. You will be disappointed when you don't get that big contract or when the business does not make as much profit as you would like, when you have to cut back for a few months, when valued employees quit and when your business is not working out as well as you had hoped. It is part of owning a business.

The main factor that causes disappointment is your expectations. If you find you are continually disappointed with the people around you, your business, and life in general, examine your expectations. If they are too high, you will continually be disappointed. Making clear and reachable goals will help you feel more positive about others and your business.

Instead of having a goal of making $50,000 this year, change that goal to increasing your revenues by 10 percent over last year. If you increase the revenues by 15 percent, change your goal to 15 percent for the next year. If you only increase your billing by 5 percent, see where you can cut your overhead or raise your prices. Make your goals realistic and you'll improve your attitude and morale.

Hold Your Tongue

Your clients will make you mad sometimes. Your employees will anger you. And you will want to get angry back. Don't. The best strategy I have found is to hold my tongue until my anger has passed. I cannot respond in a civil manner when I am steaming. I don't want to say something that I will regret or that will hurt another person. Fortunately, I work out of my home most of the time so most of my contacts are over the phone or by email.

If I know that a client is calling with bad news, I often do not answer the phone. I let the call go to the voice mail. Then I can find out the news and react before I talk to them. I can consider my options before I call back.

I also use this strategy if I have just heard bad news and I am disappointed and angry. Voice mail is wonderful, and can take my calls for a few hours while I sort out my emotions. I do not want to answer the phone and not be in control when talking to a new client. Your voice should be welcoming and open when you answer the phone. If you are angry, it's hard to pull this off.

If I am talking to someone and get some upsetting news, I often will ask if I can call them back a little later. I say I need to think about the problem and will call them in a few hours. I give myself time rather than feel like I need to give them answers immediately.

Hardly anything in life needs an immediate answer I realized. Why not give myself some time to sort out how I feel? I suggest you adopt a similar strategy and avoid that sinking feeling of "Oh I wish I hadn't said that!"

Giving Criticism Tactfully

As a business consultant, I am paid to give my opinion about other people's businesses and ideas. This requires great tactical strategy and planning. I am aware that people's businesses are extensions of themselves and criticisms must be meted out carefully. Criticism given too harshly discourages the receiver and accomplishes no useful purpose. Criticism given too softly misses its mark and does not encourage improvement. The right level and tone is an art form.

I was hired by Kathleen to help her evaluate her business marketing plan. Kathleen felt like she was drifting and not focused. She felt she should be making more money after all her years in business. She hired a Web site designer to build her a Web site to sell her handmade jewelry and paid $5,000.

I studied her Web site and although it was beautiful, it did not offer any reason for a customer to buy her product. It was a very nice brochure essentially. Her target customer was wealthy women, and the Web site did not allow them to view the jewelry from different angles. Also the Web site did not distinguish itself from other Web sites selling jewelry. And lastly, when I entered keywords in the search engine, her web address did not come up for many pages. No one would be able to find the Web site unless they already had the address.

It was a harsh evaluation of a very expensive project. I began by complimenting her on the beautiful Web site. The colors and design were truly stunning. Instead of continuing with my evaluation, I began asking her questions about what she wanted to accomplish with the site, what other sites had she looked at, and how much merchandise she hoped to sell over the web.

I found out that she expected to sell very little over the web but wanted her regular customers to have an opportunity to see her new products. She was beginning to send pieces out on consignment to her best customers and she needed a web presence to display her pieces.

I was thankful that I had not launched into criticism about her site before asking important questions. We were able to design a more effective site for her needs and change her marketing plan to use the new site to greater advantage.

Asking questions before delivering criticism is the most effective way I know to give bad news to someone. By asking questions, you can allow the other person to come to their own conclusions. In a performance evaluation ask, "How do you think you did on the Anderson project?" Often the employee will offer a more stinging evaluation of their behavior than you expected.

Temper your expectations of employees. Often business owners are hard driving people with very high expectations for themselves. Asking their employees to be the same way is not realistic. Be kind and gracious with your employees. Demand good work but be kind if they make an occasional mistake. Have them correct the error, but hold your anger as much as possible. Think of a system to prevent it from happening again.

Find and utilize the strengths in others. I once worked with a difficult woman who constantly criticized me. It was extremely annoying until I realized that she needed to be in charge of something. I put her totally in charge of one facet of the business since this was strength of hers and a weakness of mine. I told her I was depending on her to take this over and do a good job and admitted my failings. She did a wonderful job and, even though she was still annoying, she was less critical of me and was happier in her job.

Be proactive instead of "sensitive". Finding ways to highlight your strengths and the strengths of your employees while developing systems to minimize weaknesses is the essence of good management and productive companies.

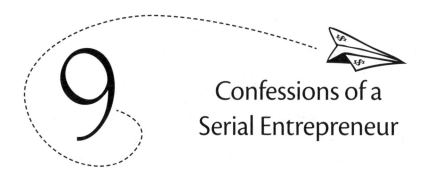

Confessions of a
Serial Entrepreneur

Milton Hershey is my hero. He started Hershey Chocolates back in 1895. Certainly he was a very successful entrepreneur. Even though we share the same birthday, September 13th and a love of chocolate, that's not why I consider him my hero.

His first business at the age of 18 failed due to lack of capital. He followed his father to the Colorado silver fields and learned to make caramel candy with fresh milk while in Denver.

Returning to New York City at age 22, he started a caramel business which failed again due to lack of money. Now penniless, he moved to Lancaster PA and started Lancaster Caramels which almost failed, again due to lack of start-up money. But a large order from a British firm at the last minute saved the firm. The company soon employed 1400 people and shipped caramel all over the world.

Here's the important part of the story. Milton Hershey attended the Columbian Exposition in Chicago in 1893. He saw a demonstration of some German chocolate making machinery and was fascinated by the process. He ordered the machinery and began making chocolate.

Milton Hershey sold his caramel business for $1 million

dollars in 1900 because his passion was making chocolate rather than caramel. It doesn't seem to me like there is much difference between making caramels or chocolate but apparently Hershey thought otherwise. He worked for years to perfect his chocolate formula and finally achieved his goal of mass producing milk chocolate. Also, treating his workers well was important to him and he followed his values by setting up schools and housing for his employees.

What a guy! Hershey could have continued with his first successful business but his heart was devoted to chocolate. I love that he pursued his interest in chocolate and took the financial risk to begin another business that sang to his soul. The lesson to me was his persistence, despite several failures and one early success, in sticking with his original dream.

You may have never had the desire to start and own a big company like Hershey Chocolate. My entrepreneurial dreams, too, were far more modest. I wanted to start a company that I enjoyed and provided a comfortable income and would allow me time to pursue other interests like writing this book, hiking in the mountains, and pursuing numerous hobbies.

Like me, Milton Hershey started up several businesses that appealed to him, learning valuable lessons from each enterprise. Milton Hershey found a business that appealed to him even though he was extremely successful in making caramel candy. My own career has morphed several times over. I try to build a new business based on what I learned with the previous business. Each business has taught me what I want to do and what I don't want to do in the future. All my businesses have threads of the previous business in the plan.

I love starting a new business! It is exhilarating and exciting. To me, starting a new business is great fun and full of expectation and promise. I think about my new idea constantly and feel energized. Designing a new business is an intensely creative endeavor. I love thinking of a new business name and finding an appropriate logo. I ask friends for their input and visit similar businesses.

This is why I have started eight businesses over the last twenty five years. Each business taught me valuable lessons and helped me make the next business more suitable to my needs. I am a serial entrepreneur. And I love helping other business people, like you, succeed. That's why consulting with clients like Judy is my next business move.

Judy is interested in starting her own business. She is married and planning to retire soon from teaching. Although she and her husband, Fred, have carefully planned for retirement, Judy feels that she would like to have a small part-time business. Judy is interested in staying busy, learning about running a business, and making some extra money.

"Marilyn, I can't figure out what business to start. I know you have had a bunch of them. How did you decide what you should do?" Judy asked.

"Well, I got started tutoring in graduate school because I needed to pay my tuition and my work study job just didn't pay enough. So I thought maybe other grad students would find my method of studying statistics useful. There were no statistics tutors so I had a great market. So I saw a need I could fill and it was very successful. It was almost the perfect business actually," I said.

"Why was it an almost perfect business? What would you consider a perfect business?" she asked.

"It was almost perfect because I had very few expenses. I made a few flyers and posted them in the grad student's lounge. I used empty classrooms for the groups. And I made about $120 an hour in 1983. It was extremely profitable. Stu-

dents called me begging to be in the group so I didn't have to sell anything. I could schedule groups when I wanted. It was great! The only thing that would make it perfect would be if I could get $120 an hour for 40 hours a week," I said laughing.

"Making money for not showing up is a dream for all of us, isn't it? That business sounds perfect but I guess you wouldn't want to stay in graduate school forever. What other businesses did you start?" asked Judy.

"In the 1980s, I got my real estate license mainly because I loved looking at houses. I took the real estate course at a vocational college for about $250 and passed the licensing test. Friends hired me to help them buy and sell their homes. Then I figured out that as an agent, I could find bargains so I started buying fix up homes. At the time, I could find a house in a great neighborhood for $70,000 so I only had to put a minimal down payment of $2,000 or $3,000. I did most of the work myself. When I sold a house, I made about $30,000 or so. Prices for houses were soaring during the late 1980s in Denver so I benefited from that trend.

"I decided I liked being a developer more than being a real estate agent so I concentrated on houses for a few years. I learned about fixing up houses in the College of Hard Knocks and made plenty of mistakes. Then I ended up being a landlord but really didn't like that business," I explained.

"Why didn't you like being a landlord? Everyone seems to be buying houses and renting them out," she said.

"I just wasn't comfortable with the giving the keys to someone for a $200,000 house and they only had to give me a $1,000 security deposit. I worked very hard on these houses and, after someone moved out, would have to paint and clean all over again. I just didn't like it so I sold the houses rather than continue renting them," I said.

"Then you were helping people do financial planning

weren't you? How did you get into that field?" she asked.

"I was writing a book about investing but realized I just didn't have the background needed to get it published. And I was advising people about simplifying their financial life. So it was another teaching type business. I liked it but to make it a growing business, I would have to get a financial planning certification. It is very difficult to find new clients and charging more would have meant I couldn't work with the people who needed the service the most. They wouldn't be able to afford higher fees," I said.

"So you opened the income tax business, right?" she said.

"That's right. I knew I liked talking with people about finances and money. I took the H & R Block tax course for $100 and worked for them part-time until I felt confident about my skills. Doing income taxes was a great way to make money. I loved doing income tax returns! I was careful to only take clients with relatively easy returns.

"And preparing taxes was valuable experience for me. I learned a great deal about tax law and loved talking with people about their finances. But it was 3 months a year unless I went for a CPA degree. I did not want to go back to school," I said.

"So now you have a mortgage company," she said.

"Yes and it is my favorite business so far and has been very profitable. I started out expecting to just do a few mortgages for my tax clients but it grew quickly and now I don't do taxes anymore. I love doing mortgages! It's actually a very creative business," I exclaimed.

"Okay if you say so. And now you are writing your book on starting a business and I'll bet you will make a business out of that too," she laughed.

"Actually yes. I have always loved talking to people about their business ideas and experiences. I have heard a lot of

stories over the last 25 years so I have a lot of material for this book. Starting a business is very creative. So I'm doing consulting with that. And I hope to do seminars around the ideas in this book. That would be really fun for me," I said.

"How about helping me find a good business?" she asked.

"You bet. Let's get started. Tell me your ideas," I asked.

As you can see from this conversation, one way to find your dream business is to constantly try new ideas. If you start a business with less than $5,000 and make an immediate income, you will not be burdened with loans and commitments. There are many low cost training programs in all major cities. Try a few different programs and learn some new skills. You may end up with a satisfying business after taking a $100 course and working for a business for a few years before opening your own company.

Some owners I have talked with now regret that they opened their business and spent significant money to get started. Often they find that they don't like their business or wish they had more flexibility to change products or services. Since they are so heavily invested in their current business, it would be a huge financial risk to change or shut it down. Many traditional businesses are not profitable for 1 to 2 years. The owners have drained their savings and cash so they feel they must make that money back.

Let's look at some other businesses. You may have had experience with one of these business models.

The Foxes Guarding the Chickens - Considering a Franchise?

When consulting with the newly laid off or early retirees, the first idea that they often consider is to buy a franchise. Since they usually have no experience in owning a company, they view a franchise as a way to learn about running a business. Franchise shows are packed with people with large severance checks who have been unable to find another job.

Even though a franchise is not a 5K business because of the huge financial commitment required, I feel I should address the prospect of buying a franchise since it is viewed by many as a good solution to unemployment and a good way to start a business. When I consult with the newly laid off or early retirees, the first idea that they often consider is buying a franchise. Since they usually have no experience owning a company, they view a franchise as a way to learn about running a business. Franchise shows are often packed with older people with large severance checks who have been unable to find another job.

The problems with franchises are (1) the franchise fees skim the cream off your profits (2) you must adhere to many rules that constrain your ability to make a profit—type of store you must rent, must buy their products and pay their price, inventory you must carry, strict standards (3) the franchise does no advertising for you generally (4) reselling can be a problem.

Franchises cost from $10,000 up to over one million dollars. Virtually all franchise agreements require the new owner to adhere to many rules. The rules may specify what type of store you must rent and it must be in a large mall. In the case of the more expensive franchises, often you must build a separate building. You must order a certain level of inventory and maintain strict standards. They will provide you with an inventory and accounting system and assist you in getting your franchise up and running quickly.

You must give a percentage of your gross sales back to the franchise forever before you pay your operating expenses. Another problem is that the franchise does no advertising for you unless you buy a very expensive national franchise such as MacDonald's.

(The Curves for Women franchise chain is a notable exception to this. To their credit they have a national TV advertising campaign and the franchise buy in is only $20,000 to $30,000.)

A customer called me seeking a refinance for his home. He had purchased a franchise for a $20,000 buy in and quit his job. He and his wife were working in the franchise. He needed to refinance his home from a 15 year mortgage to a 30 year mortgage to lower his monthly payments.

His franchise opened 10 months earlier and invested a great deal of money on equipment and their store front shop. Just now were they covering the overhead from the business but he was not making any salary yet. The franchise is in the extremely competitive field of fitness for women. In our geographical area, there are many fitness options that range from personal trainers, 24 Hour Fitness, Curves for Women, to many private workout studios and gyms. Not to mention every community around here has a public recreation center and a YMCA. The nonprofit status of the recreation centers and the YMCA makes it very difficult to compete with them price wise.

So far he was paying his household bills with savings and a home equity loan. He told me he quit a $150,000 a year job to open the franchise. As a very optimistic fellow, he was hopeful that the business would start to turn a profit soon but needed to lower his monthly mortgage payment.

Unfortunately, since his business had not been open for two years, I was unable to find a mortgage with a decent interest rate for him. Hint: if you are planning on opening a business, refinance your mortgage before you leave your job. Get a home equity line of credit at the same time.

When he told me the name of the franchise, I didn't recognize it. After giving him the bad news about his mortgage, I tried to find the franchise on the Web. I could not find a web site with this name. That doesn't mean there isn't a web site for the company but they don't seem to be promoting the brand name very aggressively if it is so hard to find.

What this does mean is that the franchise is selling their system but expecting the franchisees to build the brand name for them with their advertising. As you know from Chapter 5, building a brand name is extremely expensive. Entering a very competitive market with large monthly bills is an extremely risky proposition. It is doubtful that this couple will make any money on this venture.

This can be the reality of franchises. This couple is no doubt thinking that they can sell their franchise. However if the franchise is not making money they will not be able to sell it to another individual. The franchise company will buy it back for a nominal amount and re-sell it for the regular franchise fee.

A saleswoman, Sandy, called to sell me an ad and we met in my office. While we talked, she began telling me about her experience with a franchise. Her husband was looking for a way out of his high stress corporate job and felt that he was going to be laid off soon. He accepted a buyout from his employer rather than risk being laid off and losing severance pay.

Sandy and her husband bought a handyman franchise in a Midwestern city. The franchise fee was $30,000 per area but they also had to buy several trucks, tools, and rent an office. The franchise guaranteed a geographical area for them and required a 15% fee each month of the gross receipts. They hired handymen to go out to the jobs while they marketed the franchise and scheduled appointments.

Sandy was aware that the only way to make good money in the business was to buy the other restricted areas in the city. They were told verbally that they would be offered the rest of the metro area as soon as the company was ready to expand. Having several areas would allow them to use their trucks and employees more efficiently and their advertising would cover a larger area.

The work was hard and profits were slim. The 15% franchise fee was often most of their profit for the month. They invested over $100,000 of their retirement funds and were not making a very good income after 6 months even though they were each working 14 hours a day.

When they inquired about the adjoining areas, they were told that all those areas were sold to another person. Since the new person could afford to buy 6 areas at once, the company saw an opportunity to make a huge sale.

As a result Sandy and her husband eventually had to sell because the new owner's areas surrounded them. They had to send jobs to the new owner if the address was in his area even though the client was calling from their ad. The new owner offered them $20,000 and they had no choice but to take it.

Sandy is paying back $50,000 in loans and her husband is still out of work after 2 years.

A major problem with franchises is that they take the cream off the top of your profits. Many franchises take 8% to 15% of your gross receipts, not the net. This means if you make $200,000 in receipts in your store, the franchise takes the 8% to 15% fee or $16,000 to $30,000. Then you pay your rent, employees, electric bill, debt repayment, and all the other bills to run your business. Whatever is left after all these subtractions is your profit. And you must pay the 15% fee forever.

In addition to the 15% fee, many franchises require that you buy their products. You are not free to make a deal on soda cups for instance. You must pay their price and they often make a profit on those supplies too. If you are considering a franchise, read Chapter 10 before signing on the bottom line.

What should people consider before buying a franchise? Here are my observations and opinions after talking with many franchise owners:

- Some people are afraid of having a business. They have always worked for someone and are afraid of being out there by themselves.
- Some people feel more secure with a franchise believing that the franchise will take care of them.
- People believe that the franchise will increase their chances of succeeding at their first business. While franchise failure numbers appear low, many franchises do not count the owners who give up and sell the franchise back to the company or to someone else.
- Most franchises do no advertising locally for you. You are expected to advertise your business on your own, just as you would without a franchise.
- Franchises help you with accounting and inventory systems. Through the 15% franchise fee, you pay for services that you could buy or learn on your own for much less money.
- People think they are buying a job rather than a business. They are often disappointed in the results and the amount of money and work it takes to be successful.
- You will start off with large monthly bills. Franchises often require you to be located in a mall or high traffic location, which can be very expensive and require a lease for at least a year. Many new owners borrow the franchise fee, inventory costs, and store build out so they have a large debt to repay along with the ongoing 15% franchise fee.

- My personal reason for avoiding franchises is that I do not want to be in a store or office 12 hours a day. Nor do I want to train a succession of employees to run the cash register or answer the phone. You can hire someone to manage your franchise but it is difficult to find good managers. See Chapter 6 for more discussion on employees.
- Franchises do not allow you to deviate from their formula. You must follow their rules exactly. You cannot be innovative unless the franchise approves it.
- And lastly, how excited are you about making hamburgers or printing business cards for the next 10 years?

It is my belief that new franchisees should have business experience with a small 5K business before committing to a franchise. If you have hands-on experience with setting up your own business, you are better qualified to judge the true value of a franchise.

Are all franchises bad deals? No, some have developed outstanding brand names that get people in the door. Without an established national brand name or a truly innovative idea, your chances of success are about the same as any other new business. You will have to work as hard with a franchise as without one.

A Business in Name Only

There are a number of "business opportunities" available. These opportunities usually involve making money for someone else while you do the work. Examples are any business that depends on you working "under" someone else. The person "supervising" or "sponsoring" you gets a large chunk of your profits but rarely pays any of your overhead expenses.

My friend, Joan, is a single mom of two teenage boys. She has struggled with getting jobs that pay enough to take care of her boys. She is a talented sales person with strong customer service skills and ethics. She began in real estate four years ago and has been successful with residential sales.

"Marilyn, I am thinking of leaving the real estate business," said Joan sadly.

"Joan, I am so surprised to hear you say that. Why would you leave when you seem to be doing so well?" I exclaimed.

"Well, I am disillusioned with the real estate game. It is just not what I thought it was and I don't feel very good about being an agent anymore," she said.

"What's the problem with being a real estate agent?" I asked.

"First of all, I hate that the broker that I work for takes 40 to 50% of my commission. I got some help from her in the beginning of my career but now all I do is put that name on my business card. The company does do brand advertising but I still have to get all my clients myself and pay for my own advertising. Having a company name that people recognize is helpful but not for 40% of my pay for every house I sell or list!" she said emphatically.

"That is hard to swallow, I agree. But all the big real estate companies do the same thing. ReMax, Coldwell Banker, Metro Brokers, and even the small brokers charge 40 to 50% to work under their names," I said.

"It just doesn't seem right to me anymore. And I hate that I have to pretend that I sell a house I am listing for a client," she said.

"What do you mean?" I asked.

"You know from being an agent that listing someone's house in the Multiple Listing Service guide is what sells the house. I hate that I don't get to meet the buyers and sell the

house myself. All I do is write the MLS ad, have some open houses, and wait for other agents to show the house to their buyers. I never get to directly sell the house. It just bugs me that I have to say things to new customers like "I can sell your house at a higher price than agent X" when it is not really true," she said.

"I think you do a lot more than just write an ad for your clients such as pricing the house, helping with the contracts and getting both parties to the closing table and oversee all the details. But I understand what you are saying. It felt a little deceitful to me too when I was an agent. We help price the house and negotiate but since we never see the buyers, it is a little misleading to say we "sell" their home," I said.

"I could become a buyer's agent exclusively and just show homes to new buyers but we both know that that is not nearly as profitable as listing the home for sale. That's where the money is in real estate," she said.

"That's true. An agent can list 20 homes but can only show homes to one buyer at a time. And the bulk of the commission often goes to the listing agent, not the buyer's agent," I said.

"Since my broker has a minimum I have to pay her for each house I sell, I can't lower the percentage I charge. So I'm in a dilemma now. I'm going to have to find another job I guess. I can't continue to do this," said Joan.

"Let's think about this a bit before you abandon this career. I was a real estate agent for about 4 years. Then I was a real estate developer and bought and fixed up homes. I was a landlord for a couple of years. I didn't care for those businesses but now I am a mortgage broker and I love it. Is there another way you could use your real estate license and experience?" I asked.

"I never thought of doing something else in this field. Gee, I don't have a lot of money to buy houses so what else could I

do?" asked Joan.

"You could get your broker's license and start your own real estate agency. You have had success with real estate. It would be a shame to give up the business you have created over the last four years. You could run your business differently. And you could be more upfront with your clients about what listing their home really means. You could also cater to investors that are looking for fix up homes" I said.

"Hmm that's an idea. That's what you did with your mortgage company, didn't you? You tell the truth about how mortgages are priced. People have responded well to getting more information. And I do have quite a few investor clients. I enjoy looking for bargain houses. Maybe that's an idea I should pursue," she said thoughtfully.

"I think you should at least make a plan to start your own agency and see if it would be feasible. I'll help you get started," I said.

"Good idea. I can continue being an agent for the time being while I look at opening an agency. I want to find a different way to sell my services so having my own business might be the answer," she said.

Rather than leaving a profession she loves, Joan can find a new way to use all the information she has learned as a real estate agent. I was a real estate agent, then a developer, a landlord and now a mortgage broker. All these businesses sprung from an interest in houses and real estate. You may be in a job you don't like right now but might be able to use all your accumulated knowledge to morph into a small business that you will love.

Joan will need to do extensive research to determine if opening her own place and using her own standard of commission fees will work. Competition is fierce in the real estate business with many agents vying for customers. It is said in the business that 10% of the real estate agents sell 90% of the homes.

My experience as a real estate agent was different than Joan's. I got my license so that I could buy investment property. I was fixing up houses in the 1980's and selling them. If you are interested in this type of business, getting your real estate license will allow you to find bargains more easily.

As an agent, you can get first crack at the new listings. I would search the new house listings each day. I knew the streets and areas I was interested in because those areas would sell the quickest and at the highest prices. As an agent, I could visit the home before most people knew it was for sale. I often was buying the house before the sign went up in the yard. Bargains are easy to spot when you check an area every day.

I helped some of my friends buy their homes during this time. I enjoyed finding them bargains and was usually successful. Working with only one or two clients at a time allowed me plenty of time to search the listings for a great deal. I had an advantage over other agents since I was a psychologist and used my commissions to buy more property. I did not need to live on my real estate agent income.

One problem with being a real estate agent is that usually your business has a low resale value. The business is built on your name and your reputation. You are an independent subcontractor under another a large real estate company. Unless you are a top real estate agent, generally buyers are not interested in paying much for your client list. The new buyer would have to establish themselves with your clients. Real estate is a personality business and if the clients don't like you, they won't use you. This is different that selling a product where the client doesn't care who you are as long as they get the product.

If you open a real estate agency and supervise agents, you have a saleable product. Unless you name the agency after yourself, the business can be run by anyone.

Practice Businesses

I am a firm believer in starting a "practice business". A practice business is a small business you start with little monetary risk to practice all the basic skills you will need to learn for a large business. A practice business teaches you how to keep your accounting books, tax laws pertaining to a business, learn the tax write offs you can use, and all the record keeping tasks. Learning these skills is much easier when you are not under stress to pay lots of bills.

A practice 5K business, even if it fails, can be a great learning experience. You've invested very little money and now have a great working knowledge of business that can make your next attempt successful. That's not true of other non-5K business models in which people typically invest. These types of businesses may seriously impact your savings, require expensive loans and end up undermining your self-confidence. You may have had experience with one of these business models. The 3 main types I call: (1) a business opportunity, in which you directly work for someone else (2) a multi-level marketing program and (3) a franchise.

An example of an easy practice business is selling products on Ebay. Finding a product you want to sell is the hard part. People are going to garage sales around their homes and then selling the merchandise on Ebay. And they are making good money. Many sellers eventually specialize in a particular type of item that has made them a good profit. This is very low cost, low risk business to start. There are a number of books about starting a business on Ebay which will give you some tips and ideas.

Recently I found a resource on the Web that can help you find a product to sell either on Ebay or at a local flea market. The web site is **www.wholesalerscatalog.com** . This site has lists of wholesalers have new items at half the retail cost. The cost for one month membership is $3.95.

Be sure to do some research. Ebay has a research area that will tell you the top 10 selling items and numerous other statistics. Choose a few different items that appeal to you and check out the on line listings along with the completed sales listings. If the completed sales for the item you want to sell are not selling at a decent profit, choose something else.

If you are interested in selling at your local flea market, go to the flea market and see what booth has the most people around it. Make a list of the types of items that people are selling. Talk to the people at the most popular booths and ask them how long they have been selling at this location. You'll get great information. Choose items that are similar to the popular booths if you can make a profit after paying the wholesalers.

The beauty of flea markets is that there are no shipping costs or hassle. And overhead is extremely low since most flea markets charge $10 to $20 for a seller's space.

You will need to get a reseller's license from your state. Go to the county offices and they will help you apply for one and show you how to figure sales tax for each sale. You will get experience collecting sales taxes for your state. Give every buyer a receipt with the sales tax listed with a carbon copy for your records.

Here is another low cost idea:

Karen and Samantha met through their children who attend the same elementary school. They wanted to earn some extra money for their families while the kids were in school. After helping Karen clean out her grandmother's home to help her move to a smaller place, Sam had the idea of making it into a business.

They spent $1,000 to put ads in the local giveaway papers and a small ad in a major newspaper. They offered to buy all the contents of a home and then they would sell the items at a *garage sale. The first couple of homes were challenges in terms of bidding on the contents but they learned quickly without losing any money. Soon they had a thriving business and loved finding treasures that were discarded by the previous owner. And sometimes they found a very profitable item and made a good profit. Karen became very skilled at spotting unusual collectibles.*

The part of the business that was the hardest and least profitable was holding the garage sale. Transporting all the items, setting up the displays, and spending hours talking to browsers every Saturday was wearing them down.

In 1997, Karen was surfing the Web when she suddenly realized that Ebay was the solution to their problems. They became one of Ebay's first Power Sellers and now have a large garage space where they store and box up all the items they sell online. Sam found a buyer for all the stuff that won't sell on Ebay (as in junk!) and he comes one a week and takes it all off their hands. They sell the furniture and big items to a local thrift shop since the shipping costs would be prohibitive for Ebay buyers.

Their business is very profitable and they are considering using a service that will box and send Ebay purchases for them or hiring employees to do this tedious work. This would free them to do the work that is most profitable: spotting discarded gems in the houses they empty and negotiating with new customers. They are talking about expanding the business into buying and selling glass collectibles.

Practice your business and practice changing it to suit your needs. You will learn flexibility and compromise skills. Try to change the tasks in your business that you don't like or take too much time. Concentrate on the parts of the business that make the most money, are the most fun, and that grow your business. Saving a couple of dollars by doing a menial job that takes hours of your time is not a savings at all.

Multi Level Marketing – Caution

For many people, getting involved in a Multi Level Marketing (MLM) program is how they are first introduced to business. The way the MLM system works is that a friend signs you up to sell a product such as vitamins. You order a sample kit for $150 or so and go to their training for free. You are now in business and can sell vitamins to your friends and collect a commission on each sale. The person who signs you up also gets a small commission from each of your sales.

Julie is a friend of mine who is a tremendous athlete and a local high school coach. Like most people, she wanted to make some extra money in her spare time. She became involved in an MLM that sold organic vitamins. She called me about her new business and buying the product.

"Marilyn, you just have to try these vitamins. They are terrific and have made a real difference in my energy level. I have been playing really hard games and I just don't run out of energy like I used to," she said.

"Tell me about this product. How much are they?" I asked.

"Well, they are pretty expensive but if you get some friends to buy them, you will get a commission. The commission brings the price down a lot," she said.

"So how much are they?" I asked again.

"A thirty day supply is $89 but if you get three friends to sign up, you'll only pay about $49. That's a good deal and you have tons of friends!" she said.

"Eighty-nine dollars! You have got to be kidding! I spend less than that for gas for my car. That is really a lot of money for 30 pills. This is too expensive," I exclaimed.

"But if you get three friends and they each sign three friends, your vitamins will be free! Now that's good I think. I've signed up two people already," she said.

"How much is the commission for each bottle you sell?" I asked.

"It's $2.70 each time someone orders and you get $1.06 when the next level of signups under you orders a bottle. If I had 100 people under me, they said I'd get about $800 a month! That's a lot of money for signing up three friends, don't you think?" she said.

"Let's look at this business. First of all, your commission is only about 3% of the sale price. That is a terrible commission. Salespeople make much more than that for getting a customer and selling a product to them. Second, it is very hard to get people to buy something like vitamins especially if they are higher priced. That market is extremely competitive. A third point is that it is very hard to get customers who will keep buying month after month. Usually you have to call them constantly and get replacements when they drop out. Fourth, the company is doing no advertising for you to help you sell. They are making a tremendous profit. Most of the time, they are only paying maybe 10% commission to their salespeople and have no advertising bills. How many people have you talked to this week to get two people to sign up?" I asked.

"I guess I've talked to about 100 people. It's exhausting actually. I have to say the same thing over and over. Most people aren't interested at all and seem kind of mad at me," she admitted.

"After you talk to all your friends, who would you talk to next?" I asked.

"Gee, I hadn't thought of that. How would I get more people if my 2 customers dropped out? Everyone is sick of me talking about it already," she said thoughtfully.

"This kind of business sounds good. The idea of making money automatically is tempting. But most people drop out fairly quickly after signing up. They find it is very difficult to find new customers without advertising. And you don't make enough in commission to advertise. Spending $89 a month for vitamins is a significant bill for most people. Many can't afford it even if they wanted the product," I said.

"The company was so persuasive. I guess I got hooked with the free money part," she groaned.

"Julie, if this business was as easy and profitable as they said, do you think they would have to sell people on the concept? People would be knocking down their doors to be a part of it. The same thing is true of the all the infomercials on TV late at night. If there was a way to make $5,000 a month for "a few minutes work each day", trust me they would never spend thousands of dollars on a TV ad. And the other hook is "anyone can do this and make thousands of dollars a month in your spare time". Wouldn't everyone be doing it and telling their friends? I would," I said.

"I never thought of it like that. Those commercials are really tempting when you're looking for a solution. Thanks for helping me," she said.

The problem with an MLM is that it is not a real business. Basically you are an independent contractor to the person who recruited you. The commission you get from selling each product is too small to make advertising possible. Without an advertising budget, you are constantly recruiting your friends. The profits are only 3-10% per sale whereas a traditional business may mark up the products in the 50% to 100% range.

The most enticing sales pitch from the MLM is always how much money you can make if you sign up 5 friends and they each sign up 5 friends and so on. The pitch is that you will eventually have thousands of people working for you. You will receive huge monthly checks without doing any work because you will receive commissions from all those people selling.

The reality is that most people do not know how to sell a product and it is very difficult to find even 5 friends who will put substantial effort into this "business". It seems so easy when they are selling you on the concept but extremely hard to put into practice. There are a few people who do make this a full time job and they are successful. When I hear of these incredible salespeople who make an MLM work, I am sad. If they had put their efforts into a more profitable business, they would be millionaires with much less work.

The products are usually higher priced and it is hard to find customers who will continue to pay high prices for fairly common products. The products are often good quality but the companies sometimes make exaggerated claims.

Unfortunately many people are introduced to business and selling with MLM's. They have a negative experience and become convinced that business is not for them. They have a negative view of selling because they realize that they were sold a bill of goods. They regret the time and effort they expended in the MLM. In fact, they may be terrific salespeople but have tried the wrong system.

While you may think that MLM's would be a good practice business, they are not. You do not get the opportunity to learn skills like advertising, changing your product or services, or learn inventory control unless you are unusually successful with the MLM. Most people get discouraged and feel like they are not "good" at selling.

My advice is to start a true business. You are the boss, you name the company, you make the decisions, and you make the profit and pay the bills. Look for a business idea during your travels through your daily life. Opportunity is everywhere once you open your mind to new ideas.

10 The 5K Business Way to the New Retirement Model

The New Retirement

My dad retired at 65 after working for over 40 years as a machinist. He learned his trade in the Navy during World War II. He worked for only 3 companies over those years and his claim to fame was making parts for some of the NASA space shuttles. My stepmother worked intermittently during her life and they saved all money she made. Every dime they saved was placed into ultra safe United States Treasury bonds with the local banks. The mortgage was paid off long before they retired and they rarely had any debt, even a car loan. They saved before they bought new items.

As a result of their diligence, their retirement was "comfortable" as they put it. The Depression generation was extremely frugal, hardworking, and rarely frivolous with money. They had few fears that their pensions would disappear or that Social Security would fail to send monthly checks. The Depression had embedded a firm respect for safety in their investments. The stock market was too risky for my parents. They claimed they could not sleep at night if they had their money in stocks.

Oh how the United States has changed! The newspapers scream how Social Security seems destined for collapse. Pensions for workers are being eliminated by the most stable and profitable companies so they can show an even bigger profit to their stockholders. The 401k has become the fundamental vehicle for retirement savings. The stock market holds the hopes of many investors for a "comfortable" retirement.

Baby Boomers are changing the face of retirement. From the 1940s until the 1990s, working for a company for 30 years and collecting a hefty pension and Social Security was typical of many workers. After retiring, you played golf, started a garden and traveled. You bought a house in Sun City, Arizona and settled into a comfortable retirement with company paid health insurance and no mortgage payments.

Pensions are no longer safe harbors for retired folks. Presently only about 30% of American workers have solid pension benefits, down from 60% in the late 1980s. Many companies do not provide health benefits for retirees or are cutting the subsidy they provide.

In addition, many retirees are healthy and vibrant at 65. They want to continue to stay mentally active after retiring from their primary job. AARP released a comprehensive study in 2003 called "Working in Retirement". Of the people surveyed only 29% expected to not work at all during retirement. Over 68% expected to work at least part-time after retirement. And 16% of them expect to start their own business.

The 5K business model is perfect for many soon-to-be-retired. Starting your 5K business before retiring on a part-time basis with little or no financial risk is the perfect way to determine whether the business will meet your expectations and goals.

Forced Retirement

A company buyout of older workers is common these days. I frequently meet people in their 50s who accepted a buyout of their jobs rather than face getting laid off and losing severance pay. These highly skilled workers often face great difficulty finding a comparable job and many will never work at the same pay level again. Even though they have an outstanding resume, many find that companies are more interested in younger workers that they can hire at a much lower salary.

Worker who accept early retirement from companies with pension benefits often leave their jobs with the idea that they will collect their pensions and work for another company. In the past month, I have spoken to three people who took early retirement from management positions with the intent of finding another job. What they have found is that their college and professional education from the 1970s and 1980s is out of date. The degrees they received in 1975 or 1985 are vastly different from the course content of degrees in 2006. The younger workers are knowledgeable in areas that these workers are only vaguely familiar.

Susan is 50 years old, married, with 2 children in college. Susan took an early retirement offer after working for 25 years with a well known high tech firm. She started as an assistant programmer in 1980 and worked her way up to manager of the software division with hard work and company paid education programs. She received an MBA from a local graduate school, paid for by her firm, and was promoted in 1991 to manager of her section.

The company was acquired by a large firm and her section was merged with another. Even with her 15 years of management seniority, she was unable to secure another position within the new company. Susan was offered $200,000 as a severance and continued health benefits for 1 year. The alternative was a probable lay off, no severance pay and constant worry. Susan felt she had to take the company's offer if only for the health insurance.

Since Susan had glowing references and many offers from the company's executives to vouch for her abilities, she felt confident that she would secure another position with a rival company within 6 months. Armed with an impressive resume, Susan started an aggressive search for her new job.

What she found was that other companies were not very interested in her long tenure at one company. Some companies did not want to hire managers from the outside for low or mid level management positions. Promoting from within was a strong incentive for their employees.

Susan also found herself in the uncomfortable position of being unfamiliar with some of the new innovations in the field. Companies wanted managers for developing technology in radically different applications. Susan saw that her skills were outdated and she didn't even know the terms used to describe the new products. Interviewers used buzz words that she didn't quite understand.

After several disastrous interviews at the manger level, Susan started pursuing programming positions and felt she could pick up a staff position easily. Again she found that her skills and knowledge base were hopelessly outdated. Her MBA degree was a liability along with her title and salary as a manager. Companies wanted employees who could write programming code and had the classes and degrees to prove it.

Susan realized that she was competing with new graduates who had formal training in the new tech products and programming languages. Even though she had skills in many of these areas, her knowledge was acquired on the job and was not verifiable. Her management skills were excellent but companies would not hire her just for management abilities.

Even though Susan was highly valued at her old company, she realized that proving her potential value to a new company was extremely difficult. Much of her knowledge from her old company was acquired on the job and not recognized by a new company. She was competing with applicants who could prove their knowledge base with degrees and direct experience.

As a result of her fruitless job search, Susan is now considering a 5K business helping women in high tech positions who want coaching to promote to management. Even though she is excited about a new career, Susan misses her job, high salary, and outstanding benefit package.

Unfortunately this scenario is common. And it's not only high tech workers who are unable to find comparable positions. Virtually every job has changed dramatically over the last 10 years. While you may have been a valuable employee for your company, it is difficult to compete with applicants with new degrees in the field who have skills in all the new and popular techniques. Even if companies are not currently interested in implementing some of the new technologies, they often want to hire someone who knows the field.

When I retired at 51, I was aware that the new graduates in psychology were trained in areas that were not taught when I was in graduate school in 1980. It was doubtful that I would have been seen as a strong candidate for a position even with my many years of experience. Fortunately I was more interested in finding self employment.

An advantage of many 5K businesses for the newly retired is that you are often performing a service or task that does not require an academic degree. You are hired by your customers to provide a service or product and you either provide an acceptable service or you don't. Landscaping or installing a sprinkler system is done correctly or not. Closing a sale of a home is completed or not. Not much debate. Many former large company managers enjoy the tangible nature of their 5K business. After shuffling papers and attending seemingly endless meetings for years, producing a product or performing a service that has a beginning, middle and end is very satisfying.

The Shock of Retirement and Your 5K Business

Kathleen taught high school social studies for 28 years. Now that her three children were grown and on their own, she was eagerly anticipating retirement. She made lists of activities she was looking forward to when her days were no longer cluttered with frantic commuting and preparing lesson plans. Going to the Farmer's Market on Wednesday afternoon instead of on Saturday, leisurely reading the paper over coffee in the morning, working on her garden, and traveling in the spring and fall were things she thought would bring her great pleasure.

After the retirement party on her last day, Kathleen gathered up the last box from the classroom she had worked in for 13 years. As she walked out of the building for the last time, she saw several colleagues hurrying to the final student meetings of the year. They distractedly called goodbye to her as they walked by. Kathleen felt a pang of being left out and not being consulted about her ideas for her students. She realized she was being silly and that she did not work there anymore. Her replacement was already meeting with parents and teachers to make plans for next year. Her opinions would not be sought about this student or any other.

With a growing feeling of displacement, she walked slowly to her car. The parking lot was still full. She was free to go. Kathleen sat in her car and felt uneasy. Was retirement the right decision? Where was her place in the world now? Most of her time between August and June was consumed by teaching. What would she do tomorrow now that she had all the time in the world?

Kathleen drove home feeling like she had lost her best friend. She sat in her living room staring out the patio door.

It was a beautiful day but she just didn't fell like going out for her usual walk. Kathleen sat and wondered what was wrong with her.

You won't read much about it. It is usually dismissed by your still working friends as exaggerated. It doesn't seem to be talked about but my informal survey of retired friends and acquaintances is that there is a tremendous emotional shock when you retire. Everyone I know has reported that it is far more intense than we ever anticipated. Of all the people I surveyed about this, only one reported no negative reaction to her retirement. Everyone else reported feeling shocked, stunned, and lost especially in the first three months and the feelings were extreme. It takes about a year to find your way and be comfortable with your retirement.

Personally I was amazed at my emotional reaction when I was driving home after my last day on the job. While I was driving, I kept thinking "what is wrong with me? I should be happy. I wanted this." I felt I had lost my identity. No longer was I the psychologist. Now I was just Marilyn Sweet who used to be a psychologist. I felt like I had lost my home.

Later it occurred to me that the feeling was very similar to when I graduated from college at age 20. Suddenly I was thrust into a new world and my friends, who were living down the hall at college, were no longer available. The social structure with many friends all working towards the same goal and sharing a common vocabulary and experience had vanished in an instant. I was on my own. This working place was a place I had never been. There were new expectations and the feeling that I really didn't know what I was doing.

Retirement was the first time since I was 13 that I did not have to work to support myself. What was I going to do with all that time? Who was I going to be for the next 35 years?

I found that traveling did not have the sharp pleasure of anticipation of "vacation" that it had when I was working. Being able to shop when everyone else was at work was sweet but why did I need to avoid crowds when I had virtually unlimited hours available? I would not be able to complain about the crowds with the same exasperation as when I was working and time challenged. Listening to the morning news describe a traffic jam of commuters reminds me that I am not part of that morning throng any longer. I was thankful to be finished with commuting but talking about a traffic jam can be an opportunity to share a common experience and emotional link with my co-workers.

I was a part-time psychologist two and half days a week after my retirement for a year and it was a great way to gear down from full time. And it was a good way to say goodbye to my longtime profession. Many new retirees continue as part-time consultants in the same field. Lawyers, accountants, doctors and other highly educated professionals often have many opportunities to work in their primary field and receive very generous compensation

Putting in a year as a part-timer showed me that I was no longer interested in being a psychologist. Being part-time meant I was not part of the power struggle that goes on in every office. My ideas for the future of the organization were not sought nor did I offer any. I saw that my co-workers had the intensity for the work that I no longer possessed. It was time to move on.

The point of this diatribe is to encourage you to explore new avenues for your talents. Starting the mortgage company was absolutely the best move I could have made in retirement. While it certainly had positive financial benefits, the primary benefit was to move me away from my previous profession into a whole new arena. It has been a glorious experiment that has renewed my intensity for life and learning.

While it is probably financially positive in the short term to continue to work in your lifelong profession and set up a consultant 5K business, it is intellectually invigorating to start over in a completely new field. You may not make as much money or be as comfortable emotionally but you will meet people totally unlike those you had associated with during your working years. You will be exposed to ideas and concepts in your new 5K business that you would not have encountered if you had stayed in your field.

After about a year, I got over the shock of retirement and regained my intensity for meaningful work and added wonderful new friends to my life. My training as a psychologist has added a twist to my mortgage company. I discovered that doing therapy is a lot like helping people with a mortgage. I use the same skills but in a new way. I enjoy doing mortgages as much as I did doing therapy. What a wonderful way to continue my life!

The skills you developed during your working years can translate into a wonderful new career. Your negotiation skills and huge knowledge base as a lawyer, for instance, could be invaluable as a part time commercial real estate agent. Your clients will appreciate your unique perspective. The training that you did as a corporate Human Resource Administrator is a solid background for starting your own 5K training business in new and different skills for employees. Your new customers may hire you to develop new ideas for their company. Be creative and apply your well developed skills to a 5K business that allows you to pursue a personal interest and make some money at the same time.

Using Your 5K Business to Fund Your Retirement

Unlike franchises, a 5K business should begin making money for you immediately with $5,000 or less in financial risk. As I have said before, I recommend that you use savings to start your business rather than a business loan or a home equity loan. I have discovered that spending cash directly from my savings makes me more aware and careful of the amount of money I am spending.

My series of 5K businesses were the reason I was able to retire early. I started the businesses with very little money and when I got a payout from the business, I used most of the money to fund my retirement accounts. Having an extra $3,000 to $15,000 or so a year in income after expenses and taxes from my business made a huge difference in my financial picture.

Think of what you could do with $10,000 extra every year. You could fund your Roth IRA account with $5,000 and also your spouse's Roth IRA for $5,000. One of the best reasons to continue your business after retirement is that you will be able to continue savings in a Roth IRA or a regular IRA. The tax advantages are tremendous. You will be able to put off tapping into your retirement savings for the years that you are in business. The longer your savings grow, the better your financial picture will be when you finally stop working completely. Stretch out your business for as many years as you can.

Here is an example of how only $3,000 more per year can impact your retirement savings.

David and his wife have two children and live in a modest home. Although they knew they should be saving for retirement, they never felt they had the extra money. There was always something that seemed to eat up any extra money at the end of the month.

Now that he has gotten a new job with better pay, David saves $6,000 a year in his 401k at work. His new company matches his contribution up to $2500 a year so his savings has an immediate 100% returns. He feels proud that he can add $1000 more each year.

Since he is 46 and will retire at 66, he will have $296,537 if he earns an 8% return for 20 years on his account. If David started a 5K biz and was able to add $3,000 more a year to a Roth IRA retirement savings, he would have a whopping $444,806 when he turns 66.

My 5K businesses have helped me cope with large purchases such as cars and homes. You can save the $5,000 from your 5K biz to replace your car and get off the car loan merry go round by paying off your loan quickly. Saving for a down payment on a home or investment property is easier and quicker with a part-time business.

Of course the trick to any financial plan is to spend less than you make. This seems like a simple notion but it's notoriously hard to not spend extra money. Living below your income is one the sure way to financial freedom with or without a 5K business. One simple trick is to increase the percentage you save in your 401k IRA or Roth IRA by 1% each year. The 1% won't feel painful but over the years that extra money adds up and can make a tremendous difference in your savings. Automatic payments from your checking accounts make saving a bit easier. Just think of the monthly IRA payment the same as paying a bill. Saving for retirement is not a choice now. It is a bill that will become due.

Another benefit of a 5K business is that you may be able to sell the business for thousands of dollars and boost your retirement savings. If you have kept good records, have a loyal customer base, have acquired equipment, and used a CPA to prepare your taxes, your business will be valuable. The more data you have to document your business activity, customers, and income, the higher the price a buyer will pay. A serious buyer will want to see several years of tax returns and talk to your accountant.

Selling a business is tricky and requires contracts and clear expectations for payment. Most 5K business owners should hire an attorney or a broker with a specialty to correctly assign a value to your business. Business brokers will sell your business for you for a fee. Do not sell your business to a friend or relative without consulting a professional. Casual contracts and payment plans are difficult to enforce and you may end up with nothing so do your homework and use professionals to help you.

Extra Cash After Retirement

Start your 5K business after retirement to give you some extra cash to avoid tapping your savings. This type of 5K biz doesn't require you to make a lot of money. You may be doing something you love and money is not as important as it might be if you were still working and trying to save for your kid's college costs or your retirement.

Having an income from a pension or Social Security means you have more freedom to pursue your business as you want to and with less need to please lots of clients. You may need just $200 or $300 more each month to avoid tapping your savings.

Let's look at Rachel and her passion for quilting.

Rachel is 65 and divorced. Both her kids are married and on their own. She has worked hard all her life and wants more free time to visit her grandchildren and pursue her many interests. Rachel wants to begin making quilted items to sell in a local consignment store. Fortunately she only needs about $200 more per month to have some financial freedom and be able to travel occasionally.

She realizes that each quilted piece will take hours to make and that to price the piece based on a reasonable hourly rate will mean a very high price. Rachel is willing to invest the time and make less per hour to do a hobby she loves. Having a flexible schedule and extra money per month is worth making a minimal amount per hour to her.

Rachel figures she will need to invest $500 for material and a small website to get started. Her marketing costs will be minimal since she will be using the consignment shops in nearby resort areas.

Hobbies requiring intensive time such as crafts, woodworking, and exotic gardening will seldom pay you back for all the hours you spend to create your masterpieces. However, selling the items at craft fairs, trade fairs and flea markets may give you pleasure and some extra cash while you perfect your skills.

This is one instance where your 5K biz will not be focused on pure profit. Just be sure to make a list of the materials you used and the costs. You need to be able to price your crafts to make some profit and cover your expenses.

Thank you for reading my book. Hopefully this book has given you ideas and helped you formulate plans for your future. Running a meaningful and profitable business is a tremendous pleasure.

Visit my web site at **www.5Kbiz.com** for updated information on money saving ideas and innovative strategies from the community of 5K business owners. I have posted numerous examples of advice I have given to clients about their businesses.

Please feel free to email me with ideas, suggestions, and your business problem or success. My email is Marilyn@5kBiz.com. I love to hear from my readers and will make every effort to respond personally.

Index

Symbols

5K Business Boot Camp

- Need to talk about your idea?
- Have no idea how to get started?
- Want some help figuring out an affordable advertising strategy?
- Looking for inspiration?

As a service to my loyal readers and clients, I have started a Boot Camp to help new business wannabes test out their entrepreneurial ideas.

Check my website www. 5KBiz.com for additional information and dates.

Boot Camps are held in two formats.

1. **Teleseminars.** This boot camp consists of conference phone calls with a limited number of participants. We will "meet" by phone and discuss 5K business ideas and concepts. Each member of the group will get individual attention and help

2. **Seminars.** I will be conducting seminars in different parts of the country through conferences and workshops. The website www.5kBiz.com will have my schedule and information on how to sign up.

Need a Speaker for your Event or Conference?

I love meeting my readers! Here is a sample list of some of the topics that I would love to present to your company, group, association, or convention. Reasonable rates.

- Will Your Idea Make Money?
- Discovering Your Inner Entrepreneur
- Selling for People Who Hate Sales
- Setting Up Your Business So You Love Your Customers
- Maximizing Your Retirement Potential
- Choosing Great Customers With Advertising
- How to Be the Boss
- Coping with Success
- Requests for "Free" Stuff or How to Say No
- Developing Your Added Value Benefit Without Going Broke
- Core Marketing Ideas for Your Business
- And many others....

Also topics can be requested by your group.

Check out the website **www.5Kbiz.com** for my schedule and contact information.

Give A Fearless Guide to Starting a Profitable 5K Business to Your Friends
and
Your Nephew Camped Out in Your Brother's Basement.

CHECK YOUR LOCAL BOOKSTORE OR ORDER HERE!

Send me _____ copies of A Fearless Guide to Starting a Profitable 5K Business for $16.95 each.

Include $3.95 shipping and handling for one book, and $1.95 for each additional book. Colorado residents please add 7% sales tax. Canadian orders must include payment in US funds with 8% GST added.

Payment must accompany orders. Allow 2-3 weeks for delivery.

$16.95 X _____ number of books = $ _____

Shipping for 1st book $3.95

Additional books _____ x $1.95 $ _____

Sales Tax (Colorado only) $1.19 per book $ _____

Total Enclosed $ _____

Make checks payable to Cherry Creek Press and send to 3850 Paseo del Prado, #28, Boulder, CO 80301. Fax credit card orders to 720-294-1266

Name _____

Organization _____

Address _____

City/State/Zip _____

Phone Email_____

Please charge my _____VISA _____MasterCard

Card # _____

Exp. Date _____

Signature _____

Or order online at www. 5KBiz.com

About the Author

Marilyn Sweet has started eight businesses over the last 25 years and spent less than $5,000 each time. Her businesses have been in the areas of statistics tutoring, income tax preparation, real estate agent, research advisor, landlord, real estate developer, writer, and mortgage broker. These ventures allowed her to retire at age 51 from her "real" job as a psychologist. As a 5K business consultant, Marilyn has helped her clients begin satisfying full and part time businesses. Begin your own "5k Biz" to earn up to a 6 figure income, avoid debt, and high overhead expenses.